AND THE ANIMALS WILL TEACH YOU

AND THE ANIMALS WILL TEACH YOU

Margot Lasher

DISCOVERING OURSELVES
THROUGH OUR RELATIONSHIPS
WITH ANIMALS

B
BERKLEY BOOKS, NEW YORK

AND THE ANIMALS WILL TEACH YOU

A Berkley Book / published by arrangement with
the author

PRINTING HISTORY
Berkley trade paperback edition / December 1996

The Putnam Berkley World Wide Web site address is
http://www.berkley.com/berkley

ISBN: 0-425-15458-0

BERKLEY®
Berkley Books are published by The Berkley Publishing Group,
200 Madison Avenue, New York, New York 10016.
BERKLEY and the "B" design
are trademarks belonging to Berkley Publishing Corporation.

PRINTED IN THE UNITED STATES OF AMERICA

10 9 8 7 6 5 4 3 2 1

For Hogahn
Panda
and all the animals

ACKNOWLEDGMENTS

I thank my son, Soren, for helping me with the chapters and for giving me confidence.

I thank my brother, Dana; when it looked as if things were falling apart, I stayed quite calm because I knew you would fix it.

I thank Irene and Siena Rose for the most basic connection.

I thank my longtime, lifetime friends back on the mainland, and my friends on Kauai, for being there for me. Thank you, Janet, for help with the chapter and many things.

I thank all of the people who told me about their connections to animals and the importance of animals in their lives.

I thank President Joseph Hagan and everyone at Assumption College for their encouragement and support, and my students for their energy and insights.

I thank Serge Kahili King for his teaching of Huna.

I thank Regula Noetzli, my agent, and Jennifer Lata, my editor, for all of their help.

I thank Edgar Bourque, whose spirit is with me.

CONTENTS

AND THE
ANIMALS WILL
TEACH YOU

THE PATH OF ANIMAL CONNECTIONS

FOR many years the companion of my spiritual life was a dog. His name was Hogahn.

This didn't make sense sometimes, even to me. As a psychologist I worked with people and believed in the central importance of human relationships. As someone on a spiritual path I experienced the presence of spiritual beings in my life. But when I wanted to understand some very deep part of myself and the meaning of my life, I turned to my dog. What was I doing?

I began to struggle with this question. When spiritual understanding is at stake, we can only start with ourselves and our own life experience. I looked at the path of my spiritual development and found, to my surprise, that animals were significantly involved in my growth. They entered my life as trusted daily companions and as unexpected spiritual presences. They entered at moments when I was open to insight and change. They were with me on the path.

A spiritual journey is a journey of widening and deepening connections. Feeling connected to another being enables us to face fears, to trust, to feel safe and peaceful, to feel love. Along the path, at moments of freedom and inner peace, each of us feels the essential connectedness of all things.

We can increase our awareness of connections in many ways. Some of us are most comfortable connecting to people. Others find a sense of oneness through being with nature. Life puts certain situations in our path and we relate to them. We can discover connections through any situation that drifts, or lands with precision, onto our path.

Spiritual teachers from all traditions have spoken about the ways they have reached awareness of the essential connectedness of all things. In most of these traditions, the emphasis has been upon deepening connections to other people, to nature, and to spiritual beings. Somewhat more unusual, but present on the fringe of most traditions, is the sense of connection to animals and animal spirits. An exception is the shamanic tradition, in which animals are placed at the center of awareness. A shaman gains spiritual insight and healing power through a deep connection with animal spirits. This the path of animal connections. It is also my path.

Animals have leapt, flown, and lain across my

path since childhood. From the beginning I seem to have made connections in this way.

This book is written for those of you who love and cherish animals. I hope to show how your connection to animals is part of your spiritual journey. When you meet an animal on the path, you both are blessed.

The creatures who dwell in this book, from the rabbit in the desert to a German shepherd named Kirby, teach us how to live in the moment, how to be peaceful, how to trust, how to share strength and power, how to face fears (including the fear of death), how to heal, and how to love.

Our Western culture accepts humans, and to a lesser extent nature, as spiritual guides. Our spiritual beings tend to be modeled in our imagination by the human form. This is a cultural limitation. We are taught that the mutual trust we feel with an animal is somehow less important. We learn that the love we feel for an animal, and from an animal, is somehow less deep. We struggle with the implication that the connection we feel with an animal is a lesser connection, less spiritual or less real. I hope that these stories, my own and others, will free you of these restrictions. If you have experienced happiness and inner peace in the presence of an animal, this is your path. When you meet an animal on the path, you have met the spirit that connects us all.

Several years ago, still struggling with the question "What am I doing?" I began teaching a course in psychological theories of the human self. The students in the class were quite wonderful, and together we trudged through several theories and all of the jargon that accompanies any theory of the mind. I came away from this work with a few clear, essential ideas about the self.

First, our awareness of our self at any moment is an awareness of a feeling. Right now, at this moment, if you tune into yourself you can sense a quality of energy: perhaps you feel calm, or quietly alert, or slightly agitated. You sense a quality of energy which can sometimes be named as a particular feeling. You sense your own aliveness.

Second, this sense of aliveness, and the quality of energy of that aliveness, is at the center of the self. The core of the self is a feeling.

And third, we all have parts of the self outside of our core that play different roles. These parts take over when we need to protect our core from perceived danger. So we might act tough when inside we feel frightened, or speak politely when inside we feel anger. These parts of our self make compromises with people and society in order to survive in a demanding, sometimes cruel, environment. We develop these parts of the self in order to deal with the world and protect our center.

But our core self, that center of aliveness, never compromises. It does not play roles, it does not block feelings, it does not adjust itself to the surrounding world. We can lose awareness of our core, we can get trapped temporarily in some form of compromise, but the core self is always there for us. It remains whatever it is, from moment to moment.

One day, standing in front of the class and trying to say something meaningful about the human self, I looked out the window at some storm clouds which were gathering. At that moment I saw that when I tuned into Hogahn, or when I stood very still to watch a heron fishing at the lake, I was tuning into my core self. I was finding a quality of energy, a sense of aliveness, at the center of my self. The energy, the aliveness, was within me. But I had lost contact with it, or had trouble feeling it clearly and strongly. Connecting to animals helped me connect to my self.

The anthropologist Loren Eiseley had said this, but until that moment I was not ready to understand. "One does not meet oneself until one catches the reflection from an eye other than human," he wrote. Eiseley was not talking of the ordinary self of everyday reality. He was speaking of that inner core, the sense of aliveness that connects and vibrates with all other senses of aliveness. A student in the class, Janine, made the final leap for both of us. She said: "The core of the self is the soul."

Connecting to ourself, to our core, is the beginning of spiritual connection. When we are free to connect to ourself, we are free to connect to the universe.

Although Western culture, including psychological theory, has been mostly silent about the spiritual significance of human-animal connections, I believe we are ready for new understanding. In our culture as a whole there is a profound change in the way we are thinking about all connections. After several centuries of Western scientific categorization—the separation and analysis of parts—we are returning to the need to put things back together, to envision the whole. In disciplines ranging from physics to medicine and psychology, we are creating theories that see connections. All of this affects the human-animal bond.

While Western science was separating and analyzing, Western culture was arranging the parts into hierarchies. In a hierarchical structure, the higher thing becomes better than the lower, and as you know in our culture, humans are higher than animals. The higher dominates the lower, and justifies all kinds of cruelties based upon the higher's perception of itself as more valuable, more important, and more aware than the lower. So certain cruelties by humans to animals are accepted in our society, and the animal's pain is diminished or denied completely by the scientific theory that animals do not have feelings, do not have consciousness, are not aware of death, cannot love each other, and do not suffer and grieve.

We do not know that animals do not have consciousness, are not aware. Our culture has just assumed it, based upon a hierarchy which puts us on the top. It has been convenient for us, allowing us to build our complex structures that dominate the natural world. When the theory allows us to make other beings suffer, it is immoral.

There has always been another way of understanding ourselves and our world. It is a spiritual way that is part of all religious traditions, although sometimes it has had to go underground. It is the knowledge and the feeling that all beings are connected. At a spiritual level, at the deepest level of understanding, we are all one.

Mystical thinkers of all cultures have felt this equality, this sameness. We experience it as pain inside ourselves when we see a human child suffering, not only our own child, not only a child of our own culture, but any child. We feel a tightening in our chest, and a sense of wrongness and injustice. We experience the connection also, some of us, when an animal is in pain. When we see a horse fallen with a broken leg, or a turtle trapped without air in a net, we feel the suffering of this living being inside us. This connection is called compassion.

Our connection to other beings comes from an awareness at the core of ourselves. Sometimes, when we see a deer leaping toward the forest or a hawk gliding over the pond, we feel part of their motion. We feel the energy of leaping or gliding, the sense of bodily strength and freedom. We are connected through that wonderful feeling that comes when the body and mind are working as one. We feel that sense of inner peace that comes when the rhythms within us connect with the rhythms of animals and nature around us.

In recent years Western psychological theory has come closer to the spiritual insight of connection. In object relations theory, it was the pediatrician and psychiatrist D. W. Winnicott who said that the center of the self is a sense of aliveness. In relational theory, Jean Baker Miller said that the core of the self is a feeling. This core, this center, connects to the core of others through empathy. When we sense another person's suffering, or another's happiness, and we echo that feeling inside us, we are connected to that person's center.

Daniel Stern has studied the core self and the origin of human connections from the moment of our birth. When we are born, we cannot feed ourselves, cannot stand and walk, and cannot talk. But we have one quite amazing ability: we can tune into the rhythms of another being and echo those rhythms. In frame-by-frame and slow-motion analyses, Stern watched newborn infants responding to the bodily rhythms of their mothers. He found that they respond to some of these rhythms, such as the mother's heartbeat, even in the womb. These rhythms—heartbeat, breathing, walking, the patterns of the voice—are the foundation of feelings. When the mother is calm, her heart rate is slowed; when she is excited or upset, her heart rate increases. In extreme distress, it may become uneven. A fast and uneven heartbeat is highly upsetting to an infant whose only experience of the world has been within the safety and comfort of a steady, even beat.

The rhythms of our mother are the foundation of our sense of aliveness. We pick up a rhythm and echo that rhythm in our own body. We learn about being alive from our connection to a living being.

And the rhythms of another living being are the foundation of our knowledge of specific feelings. If our mother is usually calm, we learn that calmness, with its slower, steadier rhythms, is normal; it becomes the accepted human state. If our mother is never calm, we may lose the ability to be calm ourselves. If calmness is never echoed by anyone in our world, and we never echo it, we may stop creating the rhythms of calmness, and being calm may become a feeling that we cannot experience.

As we grow from infancy into childhood, our parents echo and accept many feelings. But they also cut off and reject certain feelings. Fear is one of the feelings that is often cut off in our society, especially in boys. A young boy gets hurt, feels afraid, and is told by his mother and father to stop crying. They will not echo his fear. He learns to hide those rhythms, pretending that he isn't afraid, and eventually he loses touch with his own feeling. Years of being told by his mother and father that fear is not acceptable make the feeling unacceptable to him also.

Stern's research deals with humans, but he suggests in footnotes that attunement—tuning into the rhythms of another being—is also an ability of "higher non-human" animals, and that animals, like humans, have a core self. Mothers already know that they and their baby connect to each other at some emotional level. And those of us who are close to animals know that we connect to animals in the same way. It is satisfying, however, to have our personal experience confirmed by work such as Daniel Stern's. Our personal knowledge is tacit, part of our awareness but difficult to put into words. Theoretical frameworks give us the language and the conceptual structures to communicate our experience. I would only amend Stern's thesis in one way: I would say that all living beings, not just "higher" ones, tune into the rhythms of the world and vibrate with them.

One of the ways we have always been able to talk about our connections to animals, even in Western culture, is through myths and folklore. In these places where we try to understand the meaning of our lives, we find animals present—animals and animal spirits. Through stories, we teach our children about their spiritual connection to the animal world.

In some shamanic cultures, when a child is born she is given an animal spirit, as a vision and a name. The child, growing up with this identification, can call on the animal's special energies and strengths. The child's spirit and the animal's spirit are one.

In our own culture we also identify children

with animals, although not with such clear awareness. We tell children stories about animals. In the
books we write especially for children, and the tele-
vision programs we create for them, most of the inhabitants are animals. We assume that children live
in the animal world.

We give children stuffed animals to be close to
and to love. When we give a child a stuffed animal,
we assume that the child and the animal will form
a special bond. The teddy bear will protect the child
from fear during the night.

And, as in shamanic cultures, we give our children animal names. When my son, Soren, was
growing up we called him Turtle. He was not slow
at all, so that the conventional meaning of "turtle"
did not make sense for him. It was long after we'd
come to know him as Turtle that the meaning of the
name became clear to us. He was highly conscious
of the space around him. He built wonderful structures, like the beautiful, sturdy enclosure of a tor-
toise's shell. Inside, he was very private. He
connected to others when he wanted, but he was
very good at slipping away.

When we tell children animal stories and give
them stuffed animals and animal names, we are
teaching them about animal spirits. And as adults,
when we make an animal part of our lives, we are
doing something quite similar to the ancient practice
of a shaman who calls upon animal spirits to heal.
Like shamans, we turn to animals for some needed
insight or healing.

11

Of course, we do not usually have the shaman's level of training and awareness. Sometimes we stumble upon an animal, seemingly by accident, who brings us the energy we need at that time in our lives. We connect to the spirit of that animal, renewing our own inner spirit. We become aware of some aspect of the self that has been lost, unacknowledged, or partly blocked by the pressures of human society. By tuning into the animal, we are reconnecting to the core of our selves. Following an instinct that, in spite of the complexity and occasional insanity of our civilized lives, we have never lost, we find the animal spirit that heals us.

In this book I have woven into the story of my own spiritual development the stories of other people whose lives have been changed by their connection to an animal. And of course, in telling these stories, I tell the story of the animals, who are also spiritual beings on spiritual paths. I try to see the connection from the point of view of the animal, as well as the human, as much as I am able.

I use the word "animal" to mean any nonhuman creature: birds, fish, and spiders as well as mammals. Sometimes I use the words "creature" and "being" to indicate that I am talking about animals and humans at the same time. I distinguish between animals and humans only in order to see, in the end, our essential sameness.

When we are deeply connected to animals, we find an awareness of perfect harmony, the natural flow between everything within and around us. When we tune into the sense of aliveness at our core, we are tuning into the life of the universe. We are part of the spirit of the universe, and at peace with ourselves.

This is the path of animal connections. I traveled this path with Hogahn and the other creatures you will meet in this book.

2

TRUST

WHEN I was a child I learned about the spirit of the universe from a jackrabbit. He taught me how to meditate. And when I felt safe enough, he taught me how to leap.

I am going to tell you a little about my childhood because my connection to the rabbit was intertwined with some of these details. But spiritual development ultimately transcends the specific conditions of our lives. You may have experienced a very different kind of childhood, yet can remember animal companions as a child who gave you the same healing insights.

When I was four years old, I got pneumonia and was hospitalized. It was a cold, rainy winter in New York City and my lungs were weakened. The next winter the pneumonia returned and I almost died. The doctors told my parents that I could not survive another winter in New York.

My parents took me to the Sonora Desert, to a small community in Arizona, to save my life. After we were settled, my father felt he needed to return to his job in New York, leaving my mother with my baby brother and me. It was a difficult time for my father and mother.

I wandered into the desert daily. Our backyard was small, about fifteen feet square, and my mother had made the entire space into a vegetable garden. She worked hard in the garden because we needed the food, but she loved the work. She was absorbed at that time in the concept of growth. I remember crouching between her thigh and a globe of squash that was fatter around than my own body, both of us awed by its size, watching it grow. She kept a record of my height in the kitchen doorway, marking off eighths of inches with a freshly sharpened pencil that she placed with scientific care on the top of my head, pressing down and leveling it to make the mark exact. The marks went higher in harmony with the squash's bulge. We grew together.

I went through the garden, a tightrope walker between measured rows of spinach and squash, to enter the desert. The garden earth was cool and fertile, rich like butter from my mother's churning. At the boundary, the surface of the ground became light and hot, with sand and desert plants stretching out toward the distant foothills. The familiar rows ended at the garden's edge, and tangled patches of camouflage lay flatly ahead. The garden was safe and humanly ordered, guarded by my mother's power. In the desert, my family self left me, and a self that was still strange came into awareness, a self that connected with all that was unknown.

I entered the desert. Looking down, I saw tiny succulents growing among the sand and the pebbles, and I moved in small waves so as not to step on them. Looking up, I saw stately saguaro cacti with great arms, and I weaved widely around them. I loved the desert. I saw the saguaros as silent, still figures, filled with wisdom and grace, lifting their arms to protect the desert and all its creatures. I was one of the creatures, and they were our guardians. I was not afraid in the desert.

In school we were shown pictures of poisonous creatures and constantly warned about their danger. These creatures—rattlesnakes, scorpions, tarantulas, black widows—lived in the desert where I roamed freely. But I was never harmed. When I was in the desert, I never even thought that one of them might harm me. I tuned into the desert and knew that I belonged there. I was one of the desert creatures, like the rattlesnakes and scorpions. Because I never felt that I was an outsider, I was never afraid. It was only at school with the human adults that I didn't belong. In the human world I had learned to feel fear.

I soon figured out that if I wanted to see desert animals moving around, I had to be with them at sunset. They would not come out in the heat of the afternoon. Fortunately, my mother was so happy to see me alive, brown from the sun and running around like a normal child, that she accepted my absences graciously. I left in the afternoon and returned after sundown, and she held supper for me.

One afternoon I had been playing in the desert for several hours and was feeling peaceful and a little sleepy. The sun's edges shimmered down by the horizon, and the saguaro shadows lay lightly on the still ground. I lay beside an old saguaro and put my head on the sand. Pressing against grains, I sleepily felt the earth's warmth move through my body and I closed my eyes.

Something woke me. I looked out at the desert, suddenly alert. To my left I saw two eyes suspended in a dark hole within my reach if I stretched out my left foot. Our eyes met for less than a second, and then the other eyes disappeared.

The next day I went back and waited. I lay down, very still, focusing on the ground. Waiting, I began to see a whole new level of the natural world. I saw a tiny spider crawling on a succulent plant, and I saw the pores in the plant, the shape of each protrusion, the way the buds pushed out from the green skin. I saw the way each tube was connected to the others. By the end of the day, I knew that plant.

The eyes came when the sun was low in the sky and the desert was crisscrossed with shadows. I felt their presence and turned to meet them. As soon as I looked, they disappeared.

The next afternoon I took my position and renewed my contact with the succulent. I watched the spider move from the center of its web to the outside in response to the slightest motion, and then return to the center. The spider was not at all afraid of me, nor was the plant. The eyes in the hole were wary.

I longed for the creature with the eyes to come out and be with me. I needed the creature to trust me. I have thought for a long time now about this need, our human seeking of an animal's trust.

When an animal overcomes its fear of us, it gives us the gift of a model that we can follow for overcoming our own fears. In human society, in our ordinary lives, we need to be able to trust. We need especially to be able to trust other humans who have power in our lives.

When an animal can feel safe with us, we are giving that animal what we would like others to give to us. With animals, especially small ones, we are the ones who have the physical power. If they are safe in our presence, we have a model for being safe in the presence of more powerful others. If an animal can trust us, we can trust the universe.

The connection of trust creates a space of safety for both creatures. Most of us have a trusting connection early in our lives, held in the safety of our parents' arms. But in the process of growing and responding to human pressures, we lose some of this trust. Some of us lose it suddenly, even violently. I did because of my illness.

I was in a New York City hospital at age four, in a room with a boy of about ten. He was sick and frightened, and his way of getting back some control over his life was to terrorize me. At night, as soon as the lights went out, he would tell me horror stories. They were not ordinary horror stories; they included the real medical terrors that he had experienced as a seriously ill child. During the day, when there were nurses and visitors coming in and out of the room, he was very quiet. I cannot remember him ever speaking, but a look from him across the beds would bring back my fear. At night, when he told me the stories, I cried hysterically. This only encouraged him, giving him a temporary sense of control over his world that his illness and the medical world had taken from him.

One day, while my mother was visiting, a nurse came and took him out of the room. I was finally alone with my mother. Whispering, feeling in some part of me that he could hear me wherever he was, I asked her if I could move to another room. Already, at four, I had accepted many of the rules of the adult world. I knew that I couldn't ask to leave the hospital, couldn't ask to stop the painful tubes that were inserted into my mouth and down my throat into my lungs, couldn't ask to go home. I never asked for anything. But I asked her to get me away from that boy. I explained that he told me ghost stories late at night and made me cry. I didn't tell her that he was terrorizing me because I didn't know that word. She didn't understand. She said that he was a very sick child and I should feel sorry for him. She didn't get my room changed.

That evening I was crying hysterically while he described some bodily torture that he said would happen to me. And then the harsh white lights came on and a nurse entered the room. I thought, for a brief moment, that the nurse had come to comfort me, that my mother had asked her to watch over me. But she lifted me unfeelingly and, ignoring my sobbing, carried me out of the room and down the hall. We got onto the elevator, and I still couldn't get my sobs under control. If she had talked to me, stroked me, done anything to show awareness, I would have responded, but she did nothing.

We got to a room and she laid me on a table beneath a doctor whom I had never seen before. He started to probe at my body with a metal instrument. I lost all control. My sobbing turned into violent shaking. He never stopped. I was a body, a pair of lungs to him. Angrily, he ordered the nurse to hold me down, and while she pinned me, the instrument entered my body.

That was the first time I dissociated. My mind split from my body and went to a space where the wall met the ceiling. I saw them working on me, and I had a thought. It does not seem to be the thought of a four-year-old, but I remember it clearly. I thought, What they are doing is wrong. Maybe they have to do whatever they are doing to my body. But if they would just pick me up first, just help me to get the shaking under control, then whatever they are doing wouldn't be so terrible, and I would be all right. But they don't know that I am here. They don't care about me, my self which is connected to my body. And that is wrong.

From this moment, I didn't trust human beings. I couldn't even trust my mother, who had not responded to my fear and had left me in the room with the boy.

My sense of trust in connection to my father was complicated. My father and I tuned into each other nonverbally, like animals, and at this level I trusted him. But my father couldn't act to protect me. My mother was the one who took me to the doctor and put me in the hospital, and the one who, if she had understood, would have changed my room. I cannot remember my father even coming to the hospital, although he must have been there.

I remember my grandfather Jake, my father's father, coming to see me soon after that night, walking with slow steps and a nervous smile across the room, holding an enormous stuffed animal, a dog. I remember that dog, white and fluffy, about two feet high, staying with me through the night and comforting me as much as he was able. I remember my grandfather holding my hands with his old hands, and relaxing a little when he saw how happy I was holding the dog. But I don't remember my father being there in the room. My grandfather never went anyplace without my father. My father must have driven my grandfather to the hospital and disappeared. He couldn't watch me suffer. You cannot open to your child's fear unless you are able to feel your own fear inside you.

So my trust in the world of human adults and, because of the boy, human children, went underground. And then, in the absence of a human teacher, the universe took over and gave me a rabbit to guide me. I found trust again with the rabbit, who came to me through an opening in the ground, a rabbit hole.

I spent several days watching the eyes appear and, as soon as I met them, disappear. Then one day, when the eyes came to the hole, I didn't move to look. I kept my eyes focused on the grains of sand and let myself feel the creature's presence. At the left edge of my visual world, the eyes were a dim blur, like a faraway star, there and not there.

I lay very still. I stayed quiet, not looking, and the eyes stayed also. They shone from the darkness of the hole, watching me.

Before the eyes had arrived I was restless, and my mind had to tell my body to keep still. My foot itched, my leg stiffened under me, and my eyes darted around for something to hold them. I was looking for something to absorb me.

As soon as the eyes appeared, my body stilled. My mind did not need to try to control it. When I felt unified with the rabbit, I felt unified within myself. The rabbit and I were anchored there in harmony.

Other creatures, like the little spider, could create this stillness in me, but with the rabbit the feeling was deeper and longer. Time stopped, and I just stayed.

His nose came out of the hole first, twitching. He was gathering every possible molecule of smell to understand me. I became even more still. My body knew instinctively what to do. My heart rate and breathing slowed their rhythms and were steady. The smells from my skin, my breath, my hair were smells of calmness. When he had sniffed a complete image of my energy, he stuck out his head.

Then in one graceful motion his whole body was outside the hole. He emerged totally in charge, totally together, and sat there with me. I don't think he would have sat next to the hole for so long if I had not been there. He kept me company for a long time.

Then, in a stirring of energy that seemed to come from both of us together, we moved. I shifted my weight and stood up slowly, while the rabbit took several light hops away from the hole toward the western sky. The sun was still reflecting rays from its position below the horizon onto the cirrus clouds that sat like rows of thick beige lamb's wool on a loom. Gathering momentum, the rabbit loped westward. I had an image of him leaping forever into the womb of the sun.

One day, when I was almost a year older, there was no school and my mother was taking my brother to see the doctor. She knew how I felt about doctors and allowed me to stay home. It was still early when, holding Dana on her hip, she waved good-bye. I was in the living room on the sofa, and through the window I could see the mountain, shadowy purple and tall, and below it the brown and green mounds we called the foothills. At that age I took the word literally, thinking of the little hills as the many feet of the giant mountain. I didn't have a plan, but I knew I was going to visit those feet.

This mountain, which loomed on the southern horizon of our town, affected our lives deeply. It gathered drops of moisture that clustered into clouds, keeping the clouds like baby birds in a nest until they had time to form. The fierce desert wind could not blow them out of the nest. They settled against the mountain, protected. When it was time, the mountain sent the clouds out over the desert, giving it rain, making it lush with cacti, lizards, rabbits, spiders, snakes, and all the other creatures who needed water to stay alive.

The peak was majestic and, except to mountain creatures, uninviting. But the foothills rolled beneath like a calm ocean, asking you to enter. The people who lived at the edge of the foothills talked about them with affection. Men went on horseback to collect plants there and to hunt.

Without a horse, I never actually got to the

giant's feet. After walking for several hours, I reached a deep, soft-sand trench, an arroyo. As a desert child I knew about arroyos, dry riverbeds that could flood suddenly and wildly from the storms that came out of the mountains. I looked across, and I could see that after more desert flatness the land began to slope gradually upward, the beginning of a foothill. But it didn't look like a neat little mound anymore. It was too big up close, like looking through a magnifying glass; there were rocks and bushes in patches of confusion, but no overall sense of form and containment. I needed to rest.

The rabbit had taught me about stillness so well that I now did it naturally. The arroyo was lined with large rocks, and I chose one with a flat smooth side facing the riverbed and leaned against it. My body was comfortable and my mind was quiet, and I just stayed there in the riverbed. It was a new kind of space for me. The space flowed between banks like the river in New York where I used to walk with my father. The sand was deep and soft, like the beach where we went on Friday nights, eating pots of steamers with buttered rolls in the restaurant that sat on stilts on top of the water. I sat in the middle of ocean sand and river shape, but everything was penetratingly dry. There was no water. I sat there trying to absorb this.

I fell asleep and dreamed of water. Slow rolling waves were lifting me gently and putting me down again in the blue sea. I was floating with a big brown seal I used to visit in the Central Park Zoo. I had one arm around his body just below his head, holding on to the thick rough scruff of his neck, his flipper resting lightly on my side. He looked like my father. We rolled on the waves.

In my dream the seal and I heard a strange noise, a cracking sound. We looked up and saw a seagull hovering over the rocks on the shore. It had dropped a clam from its beak onto the rocks, breaking the shell. The gull swooped down and retrieved it.

There was another crack, and this one woke me. I opened my eyes, expecting to find myself at the ocean in New York. I saw the sand and the rocks at the edge, and my eyes followed the rocks, trying to recognize this shoreline. And then I saw it, perhaps twenty feet upwind: a brown shape moving part of itself, anchored in place beside a rock but shifting regularly from left to right and back with a quick motion. I had slept through the afternoon and it was late and the light was low and tricky. I wasn't sure what I was seeing.

Then the shape clicked into recognition: it was an animal crouched beside a rock with a rabbit in its paws. I could see the rabbit's long ears flopping on the sand. The animal was moving its head to pull apart the fur. The crack came again. Its teeth severed the rabbit's bone.

I watched as he ate the rabbit. He was a small, thin coyote, an animal I had only seen before in pictures. I went into a light trance, distancing myself. I felt myself first as the rabbit being torn apart. I was not really there—my body was there, spreading out into the surrounding space, hanging together by a strand of skin, and then by just the energy connecting the separated pieces. I felt no pain. My spirit was floating calmly, watching my body merge with the coyote and the universe.

Then, without any conscious transition, I became the coyote. I was hungry and the rabbit was warm and delicious. I could feel the happiness in my body as the rabbit entered and, dissolving inside, gave me energy. I could feel my body singing with strength.

I came out of the trance and looked again at the coyote finishing the rabbit. He licked his paws delicately, flawlessly. He licked the rabbit's pure blood from his nose and lips. Then, probably because I was no longer in the trance and he was no longer devouring his rabbit, he saw me. I could see the startled response of his body, the widening of his eyes and the raising of his ears. I could feel his moment of fear; it went right inside me, and I felt afraid too, each of us entering the other's sphere of awareness.

Then we both relaxed. We were, after all, about the same weight and neither was going to eat the other. He rose and stretched nonchalantly, telling me he was cool. He turned his body, showing me his flank, but his head pivoted so that his eyes could stay with me. When he was certain that I wasn't going to chase and pounce, he tossed his head and, turning away decisively, sauntered off. I felt suddenly lonely. I felt as if he had been my last friend and I was alone in the universe.

Somehow, during my trance and his feast, the sun had set. It was going to be dark in about an hour. I jumped to my feet, back to the ordinary world. I bent down and tied my shoelaces tightly, making my feet secure. I started walking, then trotting, then walking, in a smoothly alternating rhythm, quickly and lightly over the desert sand, moving always toward the north, taking detours around rocks and saguaros but returning to the glow from the western sunset on my left, moving toward home.

But I was more than an hour from home, and I knew that. I was in the desert, and I wasn't frightened, but I was alert. I didn't know this part of the desert. But if I could reach the rabbit hole by dark, I knew I would find my way home.

I watched the bright red of the clouds in the west go to purple. As I ran along, I saw the distinct shadows of the saguaro merge into the darkening stones and sand. The purple sky deepened to a pervasive gray, and the ground became gray also. I was running in grayness.

And then I was running in darkness. I could no longer be sure that I was heading north. The guiding mountain had disappeared in the dark sky. I remembered the stories of children who followed the moss on the forest trees to lead them north. But the desert had no trees and no moss. I wondered if by touching the saguaro I might be able to feel a difference between its north and south sides.

I stopped and put my hands on a wide old trunk. I touched it gently at first, then pressed my fingers into its rough side firmly, moving around it. It seemed equally rough and windblown on all sides. But touching it comforted me. Then I looked up and remembered that the arms of the saguaro were often lifted on an east-west axis. I moved ahead so that the arms stayed on either side of me, perpendicular.

And then there was a glow on the horizon to my right. As I walked, the east brightened into a ball of calm light. I had been given the full moon, rising in the east.

I reached the rabbit hole with the aid of moonlight. I approached from the south, where the rocks formed a boundary. Before I could even see beyond the border of rocks, I heard drumbeats. It was many drums, each one gentle and soft, but together forming a great circle of sound. I stood still and listened. When I had absorbed the rhythm, I lifted my right foot, and stepping in time with the beats, I moved up to a rock at the edge of the clearing.

There I saw an incredible gathering of jackrabbits, leaping into the air and landing on their great paws, drumming with their bodies under the full moon. They leapt up and down, rising together in small clusters at slightly different starting times, so that some bodies were always suspended in midair, at the height of the leap, and some were at the end of the descent, paws thumping the ground. The dancers rose into the air in great leaps and sank back into the ground with deep bendings, unifying earth and sky with their motion. The dance kept going, like Navajo circling and Sufi twirling, repetitively and hypnotically, the dance of the jackrabbits.

I watched in awe, losing track of time, and eventually the dance ended, with the rabbits quietly dispersing into the desert. I picked myself up and headed toward home. The moon was sending down acres of light and I knew this part of the desert intimately, and I was safe. I was filled with a sense of joy and calm from the rabbit dance, and I walked almost effortlessly over the ground.

When I reached my house, all the lights were on and there were strange cars and trucks in the driveway. Male voices rose from the open windows. It was only then that I became nervous. I was afraid to go inside and let them know I was all right. I crouched in the garden, my heart pounding. Then my mother passed by the kitchen window, with her hair falling loosely over her light blue blouse, and I ran through the kitchen door and into her arms.

Claudio Naranjo and others who have written about meditation define it most simply as focusing. Complete focus brings a quiet to the mind that takes us out of our ordinary clutter and into a world of nonordinary reality.

The rabbit taught me to focus. He taught first, as any good teacher does, by example, watching me for hours with his eyes.

He taught me by holding my attention in the present moment. Everything was there for us: the desert, the sky, the motion of the air and the lengthening shadows, and our connection to each other. There was no need to go into the past or the future for anything.

And he taught me to leap. He taught me to take chances, to move through space with lightness and joy, to jump without fear, because at the center of that leap is the stillness of freedom and peace.

I carried the image of the rabbit's leap for the rest of my life. The rabbit took two or three small hops and then one large leap. The smaller hops were preparations, like the run preceding a basketball jump shot. The jump itself was magnificent, both long and high. It stopped time, ordinary linear time. Like a basketball player or a deer in flight, the rabbit was suspended in time and space for that instant at the center of the leap, when he was not rising higher and had not yet begun his descent. He was motionless at the center of the great leap; the stillness at the center of great motion.

After we moved back to New York, I studied that rhythmic structure in dance, doing grand jetés across the floor of Ella Dagonova's studio. I slowed it down into the motions of glide and balance in ballet and in my own dances. This rhythm underlies all our motion as we move across space, covering ground. The ground in the natural world is not always even, not always smooth. We leap over stones, fallen trees, holes, and patches of water. Dogs and horses leap over human fences. Most of all, we run and leap for joy. At that moment of stillness at the height of the leap we are free. Gravity has lost its hold on us. Time and motion stop their pull.

This stillness at the center of motion is the same stillness that is present at the center of emotion. The heart of great energy is the calm of unmoving. This is the Taoist concept of emptiness; the Mexican Indian concept of nada. It is the center of bodily motion, the heart of emotion, and the core of our soul.

The jackrabbit in the Sonora Desert taught me all this. He was just a rabbit and I was just a child. Each of us, in our own way, opened ourself to this knowledge.

Many years later, a shaman taught me to enter another world where an animal would guide me to deeper understanding. Looking back on my time with the rabbit, I see that the world of the desert at sunset was that world of nonordinary reality. I didn't think of it that way; I didn't know these words or concepts. But I did live them. With the rabbit as my guide, I learned to let things happen and wait receptively for whatever came. I learned that when I was open, there were infinitely many things to sense and relate to—the air, the sun, the shadows of the sun, the slight changes in the air as it passed over my skin, the slight changes in the shadows as the sun imperceptibly moved toward the horizon. I saw the tone of the sand deepen as its grains reflected the light more from the side than from above. I saw the saguaro go from its weathered daylight skin, with all its pores and healed-up gashes, to a huge silent presence, a massive protector in the desert night. I learned to trust because I was so safely connected. I trusted the universe and was happy and free.

I fit myself into the rabbit's world, just as later Hogahn fit himself into mine. But it was always a relationship. Once you see things as relational, everything is a relationship. The rabbit was aware of me, paid attention to me, let our energies flow between us. He accepted our connection. He taught me how to fit into a strange world, but his world was changed by my fitting, and on his part, he learned to let me fit.

When he sat there with me, just sitting, there was a level at which we merged. We were part of each other, and the feeling expanded to include all of the spiders and lizards, the succulents and saguaros, the stones and sand, the air and sun.

I must have needed that sense of oneness to heal myself, and I could not have gotten it from humans at that point in my life. The rabbit taught me to reach the peace inside myself.

I was a child, and I could see wisdom in animals and plants and the desert itself without prejudice. I was able to connect to the spiritual wisdom within my own being through their reflections. They opened themselves to my spirit and sent my spirit back to me, clear and strong. We were one beautiful, peaceful whole in the shining desert.

STAYING CONNECTED

WHEN we experience a deep connection to any being—spiritual, bodily, or both—we know that the
other being has touched our core and we have
touched theirs. We know that we are not separate.

But all of us, at some time in our lives, have
opened our heart to another person and been hurt.
There is risk in the opening of one self to another.
Relationships bring us many wonderful things—
love, happiness, and a sense of belonging—but the
ground supporting the growth of these things is our
trust that we will not be harmed.

The Dalai Lama once said:

> All of Buddha's teachings can be expressed in two
> sentences: "You must help others. If not, you should
> not harm others."

And Isaiah wrote:

They shall not hurt nor destroy
In all my holy mountain.

Not-hurting comes naturally to humans when there is spiritual awareness. And not-hurting comes naturally to animals. Animals, instinctively and naturally, do not harm. I am speaking here of emotional harm, hurt to the mind and spirit; in other places I will talk about bodily death, and human and animal violence. Now I am talking about the soul. In human relationships, we sometimes hurt each other's souls. In our relationships with animals, our soul is not harmed.

Why don't animals hurt us? I have thought about this question for a long time, and I know that the answer for me must make sense on both an emotional and a spiritual level. I call my answer *the principle of staying connected*. Animals do not hurt us because they stay connected.

To explore this principle, I would like you to imagine that you are sick and feel a need to be comforted. We are going to look at three possible beings that you might go to for comfort, the moon, a human companion, and your dog. I'd like you to imagine these possibilities with me.

In the first case, you are feeling sick and you go outside to look at the moon. You open yourself to its beautiful shape resting in the middle of the dark sky, and the grace of its light. You feel energy and peacefulness from the connection, and you are comforted.

Now a cloud blows over and covers the moon. Can you sense how you feel at this moment? You might want the moon to come back into view; you might wait for the cloud to pass over. But you wouldn't feel that the moon is turning away from you. You wouldn't feel rejected by the moon's disappearance. You are not hurt by the moon.

In the second case, you go to a human companion for comfort. You tell your companion that you are sick and feeling down. You hug each other if that is part of your relationship. Your companion talks soothingly to you, accepting your feelings. You connect to each other and you are comforted.

But imagine that your companion does not respond, or says something in a tone that feels defensive, impatient, or angry. You feel hurt. You are picking up empathically that the person is putting up a boundary, closing you out. The hurt enters when the other person breaks off the connection.

In the last case you go for comfort to your dog, who is sleeping on the sofa. You sit down next to him and hug him. He thumps his tail in acknowledgment and continues sleeping. You feel more peaceful, more grounded, and you are comforted.

Now imagine that your dog gets up from the sofa, stretches, walks around, and lies down on the floor. If you are feeling really down, really needing physical contact, you may feel sad for a moment. You would have liked the dog to stay next to you. But most of the time you will still feel connected to him from across the room. It would be very rare to feel that the dog is rejecting you by moving away. You do not feel hurt.

This is the major difference between human and animal relationships. You do not pick up from your dog a defensive feeling that your presence is not wanted, or that your need for comfort is threatening. You do not pick up these feelings from the dog because *the dog doesn't feel them*. The dog may have moved away because he was too hot, or his leg was cramped and he needed to stretch. Often a dog hears noises which we don't and moves to a place where he can pick up the sound more clearly.

Many psychologists would say that you are projecting onto the dog only positive feelings and projecting onto the human only negative feelings—that it's all in your mind. I am not denying that we project feelings from past experiences onto the present. But that explanation is overused in our culture. The experience of correctly picking up the feelings of other creatures needs to be seriously acknowledged. Our experience of staying connected to the feelings of others—positive and negative—needs to be validated. We are able to tune into feelings with accuracy and clarity. When we are not closing ourselves off, we empathically sense another's feelings with exquisite knowing.

Animals do not close themselves off to other creatures' feelings. They accept feelings, as they accept smells, sights, and sounds, as parts of their world. They defend themselves by letting in all of their perceptions in order to find out as much as possible about the situation. A smell tells them that a human creature is approaching; a quality of energy tells them that the human is tense—angry or afraid—and therefore dangerous. They do not defend themselves by disconnecting. They remain open to feelings just as they remain open to smells and sounds. They stay connected.

This is an incredibly important difference between animals and humans. Animals remain open; humans shut down. This is why humans hurt us and animals do not. We are hurt, ultimately, not by the feelings, but by the closing off of the connection.

Animals are someplace between humans and the moon. Like humans, animals have core emotions—fear, happiness, and inner peace. But like the moon and the rest of the natural world, they do not have any of our human verbal and social structures that teach us to defend ourselves by separating and closing off.

I do not think that animals are incapable of closing off. I have seen them do so when they are sick and withdraw into themselves to heal. And I have seen animals pretend to close themselves off as a strategy for dealing with humans. We have all seen dogs ignoring, or more accurately pretending to ignore, our requests. They don't obey us when we tell them to get off the sofa, but they almost always give away the fact they are listening to us—by moving their ears, turning their head away to avoid eye contact, shifting some part of their body. They may not do what we want, but they stay aware. They just pretend that they haven't heard. One day when Hogahn and I were at Lake Chauncey he gave me a wonderful example of staying connected.

It was summer, and we had a pattern of hanging around the house until midafternoon and then going to the lake. We stayed on the beach as long as we were comfortable, usually until after sunset. When I was ready to go, he was ready also. We always left for home tired and happy.

One day each week I went to my office at the college. I had meetings with students in the morning and taught a course in the afternoon. By the time I got home it would have been too late to swim, so that day we went to the lake in the early morning. That one day each week my mind was on getting to school, preparing for the class, and seeing students who had asked for help. At the lake, I just wanted to swim and leave quickly.

Hogahn was unhappy with this change in our pattern. As soon as we had gotten into the water and were beginning to enjoy ourselves, I would insist on leaving. He would drag on the walk back to the parking lot, and when we got there he would look back at the water, find things on the ground to examine, and do anything to delay getting into my truck. But Hogahn had been very well trained as a puppy by a friend, Laura, and I could count on him to eventually do what I needed.

On one of these days I had given myself just enough time to drive home from the lake, change, and make it to school for my first appointment. I had a Toyota pickup and Hogahn had to jump up into the bed. Soren, or any strong person, would have just lifted him into the bed, but I wasn't able to do this. I had started swimming about ten years ago in order to heal a ruptured disk in my lower back. I could not risk reinjuring the disk by lifting a ninety-pound dog.

We stood side by side at the back of the pickup and I told Hogahn for the second time to get in. He stood there pretending not to hear me. I told him again, increasing the sternness in my voice as he looked off into the distance, his large, heavy body planted solidly, unmoving.

A sense of desperation suddenly and unexpectedly came over me. It was a very unusual moment: I was flooded with a feeling of helplessness that I rarely experience. Without any prior thought, I fell to my knees and threw my arms around Hogahn's neck. I loved him, and in my desperation my instinct was to seek help from him, even though at a logical level this was contradictory since he was the immediate cause of my difficulty.

With my arms around him and the weight of my upper body pressing against his neck, he broke loose with a powerful thrust and leapt into the truck. It was an amazing burst of energy—he had to break my hold on his neck at the same time that he was propelling himself upward into the bed. It was as if the energy of my desperation had entered his soul and he'd acted instantly, doing the one thing which he knew would help me. I immediately felt calm and balanced; I thanked him and drove home.

When Hogahn leapt into the truck, he was not only helping me; he was restoring harmony to both of us and to the space of our connection. In a wider, very real sense, he was restoring harmony to the world, our world. My desperation and imbalance had become his imbalance also, and the imbalance of our world. When you are connected to another creature, her pain and happiness is your pain and happiness. Animals know this. Humans know too, but we block our awareness.

Empathic awareness is a natural perceptual ability, like vision and touch. Empathy is attunement to the vibrations of energy in the world around us. If we are humans, we identify certain frequencies, certain qualities of energy, as specific emotions. Other qualities of energy, such as the rhythms of waves lapping the shore and the reflecting light of the moon, are perceived by us without being given names. We sense them without needing to label them.

We are aware of qualities of energy all the time, at every moment. We are continuously connected to the energy of the air around us, which we bring inside our bodies with every breath. The air brings waves of energy which we experience as sights and sounds. There is a continual, interactive relationship between the energy of our bodies and the energy around us. When the wind blows over our face, or a sound comes to our ear, our body takes that energy inside and vibrates in connection with it.

In a book on empathy and compassion, I said that empathy is "touch at a distance." The perception of touch on our skin and the perception of a feeling are highly similar, bodily and emotionally. The philosopher Raimundo Panikkar said:

> The touching point, you see, is a point which does not separate one thing from another.

When someone whom you love and who loves you touches you, the feeling of connectedness and well-being can spread through your body in a flowing wave. This wave can happen empathically, without the actual contact of skin against skin. It can happen when the person is spacially a few inches away, a few feet away, or across a ball field. One of the closest connections I ever felt with another person happened on a dark winter night on a baseball diamond. A friend and I were walking around the diamond, measuring the closeness of the bases and our own closeness. I was on first base and he was on third, about 127 feet apart, when we felt a wave of connection.

Animals accept empathic awareness exactly as humans accept visual awareness, as snakes accept their awareness of bodily heat, and as dolphins accept sonar waves. It is part of their world.

Humans seem to be the only creatures who block awareness of specific energies. Some experts say that historically we needed to block awareness of emotions in order to create the kind of human structures, the civilizations, in which we live. If we are not dealing with feelings, we can focus on intellectual and organizational concerns.

I was once at a business meeting of ten very intelligent, usually sensitive men and women. Two of the men had an argument over an organizational issue that became personal. They started screaming at each other, and one of the men, unable to speak and with tears in his eyes, ran out of the room. After a brief moment of shocked silence, everyone proceeded to talk as if nothing had happened. Men are not supposed to cry; they are certainly not supposed to cry at a meeting; and everyone tried to deny that anything had happened. By blocking our feelings of confusion and upset, we had the time and focus to complete the business of the meeting and keep the organization running efficiently. But think of the cost to our selves, our feeling of trust, and our sense of belonging. Think of the energy it required for us to block our feelings and pretend that nothing had happened.

Animals simply do not do this. Perhaps that is why dolphins, who are probably as intelligent as humans, do not build skyscrapers, do not have private property, have not yet created medical schools. They have not focused their intelligence in this way. They have kept their intelligence intimately connected to all of their other awarenesses, so that awareness of sadness is just as important as awareness of sound.

Animal and human perceptual systems rest in the safety of harmony and stability, and are instantly active in the presence of change. Change in the context of a stable, harmonious world means the possibility of instability, imbalance, and danger. Our animal-human bodies respond instantly to change.

When the world around us is relatively constant, we can cease paying attention. On the Hawaiian island of Kauai the wind blows steadily from the east. It is only when the wind stops or changes direction that everyone pays attention.

Change occurs all of the time in the natural world, but it usually occurs gradually, allowing our bodies to adjust. The sun sets with ponderous slowness over the western ocean of Kauai, and our eyes have as much time as they need to adapt to the change from yellow brightness, to deep reds and purples, to shades of gray drifting into darkness. When a storm approaches from the north the wind changes from east to west and the ocean begins its slow swell. Turtles, dolphins, owls, and fishermen all know these signs, and their bodies prepare for the storm. When we are aware, we respond to the change by our own changes, making fine adjustments to bring us back into harmony with the whole.

When a change occurs suddenly, our bodies respond with a startle. Our heart speeds up, our breath quickens, and our whole nervous system jumps to attention. A sudden loud sound entering the harmony of a stable world produces a startled response in all of us. And any new sound, even a whisper, produces an immediate alertness and focusing of our attention. When we think we are alone, and we hear the slight crackle of something stepping on dry leaves, we listen with all our attention. The animal-human body becomes instantly alert. Our bodies respond quickly to the quick changes and slowly to the slow changes; we stay connected.

When the animal-human body responds empathically to feelings, the same thing is happening. We are staying aware, adjusting to the change, bringing ourselves into harmony with the whole. We act to restore the stability and safety of our world.

In shamanic understanding, everything is energy. The bodies of stones and our own bodies, the wind and the moon, are all qualities of energy. Carlos Castaneda studied with Don Juan, a shaman, and preserved his teachings in words for us. Don Juan says:

> The most difficult part about the warrior's way is to realize that the world is a feeling.

When we are really aware, we see a world of energy. But how do we experience energy? We know it as feeling. We too are energy, and we connect to any being by vibrating with that being's energy. We tune into the energy and receive it as a feeling inside ourselves. If we stay connected, an adjustment happens between the energy and our self, and we come into harmony with each other.

Penelope is a sheep who sensed a change in her human companion, Joannie, and acted to restore the harmony between and around them. By staying open and acting on her knowledge that something was wrong, she literally saved their connection.

Penelope is one of several ewes, rams, and horses who live on a farm with Joannie and Bob. It is a beautiful farm, set on level ground with a steep green hill behind the barn. There are fruit trees, berry patches, and vegetable beds, and Bob's cousin Charlie grows hops for his beer on vines that hang like honeysuckle from the garden fences. Bob is just finishing a studio near the chicken coops where he does his pottery. There is a wonderful feeling about the place; everything has a sense of function and comfortable harmony. But in order to keep their farm, both Joannie and Bob have to work at outside jobs.

I watched Joannie late one Friday afternoon, after a hard week at work, go out to the barn to care for the animals. She opened the stalls first, putting food out for the horses and ewes, then separately for the rams. As she moved about she talked to each of them, greeting them by name. They responded to her happily, eating a little, going over to greet her, eating some more. While they were eating, she went around opening various gates, and when the horses and ewes were ready, they wandered out to the pasture. Then she raked the stables, shoveling manure into a wheelbarrow which she rolled up the hill about fifty yards to a compost heap. She left the gate open so the ewes could follow, and they chomped at the plants alongside the path. I noticed that the largest of the ewes was especially attentive, watching Joannie as she moved between barn and hill, following her with her eyes.

When Joannie was finished cleaning, she called each of them; the largest ewe, responding to the name Penelope, trotted back through the gate into the barn area, followed by the younger two ewes. I was impressed. Penelope's continual awareness of Joannie's movements reminded me so much of Hogahn. After the ewes were safely in the barn, and she had let the rams out to the pasture, Joannie told me about Penelope.

Penelope has been with Joannie since she was a lamb, and Joannie helped Penelope deliver both of her own lambs, so there is a real closeness between them. But Penelope is not physically affectionate. Some sheep, Joannie said, will come up to you to be rubbed and petted, and others, like Penelope, like to keep their distance. Penelope kept the connection to Joannie with her eyes.

After Penelope's lambs were born, Joannie noticed certain traits in her offspring which, while not bad, were not completely desirable in Jacob sheep.

Joannie takes the breeding of this unusual kind of sheep seriously, and she started to think about selling Penelope. She didn't have enough room to keep her and get another more breedable ewe.

But Joannie was upset about the idea of selling Penelope. She began to act upset when she was around Penelope, and even more upset when people who were interested in buying her came to look. At this point, Penelope suddenly started to rub against Joannie, pushing her head against her thigh to be petted, staying beside her. It was as if Penelope were literally holding on. This made Joannie feel even worse about getting rid of her. She decided to keep her. Joannie relaxed, the buyers stopped coming, and Penelope promptly reverted to her normal, mildly aloof self.

Penelope was physically affectionate only when she sensed she was somehow in danger—or, more accurately, when she sensed that she *and* Joannie were in danger, because if Joannie was upset, there had to be something wrong in the space they shared. This is the essence of empathic connection. When something is wrong, the feeling is there for both beings. They are in danger together.

We do not know what Penelope was thinking, whether she guessed that the people who came to look at her were going to take her away. It doesn't really matter whether she grasped the human situation, the ownership of animals and the buying and selling of them as objects. She knew that something was wrong, that there was imminent danger, and she acted on her feelings. She acted precisely in a way that stopped the danger—her separation from Joannie—and saved their connection.

Penelope and Hogahn knew that they had to be in harmony with the world around them. They knew that harmony is the natural state of the universe. But the world is always changing, and some of these changes bring danger and disorder. Their instinct was to face the danger and restore order.

The one thing that we need more than anything else is to stay connected. Harmony depends upon being connected. When we are connected to the ground beneath us, to the air around and within us, and to the creatures moving across our field of vision, we are in harmony with our surroundings. And as we expand that sense of connection, to the moon and stars, to the spirits, to visions of other realities, we are in harmony with the universe.

Being close to animals and experiencing the world as they do has taught me about harmony. They do not shut out their surroundings. They do not close themselves off to sights, smells, and sounds. And as naturally as they open themselves to the surrounding sounds, they open themselves to the surrounding feelings. They let in the vibrations, and resonate to the energies around them.

Rupert Sheldrake's work on animal telepathy gives us another view of the powerful ability of animals to stay connected. Sheldrake tells about animals who know when a family member is coming home, and go to sit by the window or gate to wait for him. In most cases the animal begins waiting at just the time that the person is leaving for home.

Hogahn used to do this with me. My neighbor Speed told me that a half hour before I arrived home each day, Hogahn would walk up the hill to the top of the driveway, where he had a clear view of the incoming roads, and lie down. My hours were not regular: sometimes I left campus immediately after my last class and sometimes I stayed for meetings with students or faculty. I could arrive home anytime between two and six. But the drive from campus to home was one half hour, the length of time Hogahn waited at the top of the hill.

When Speed told me of Hogahn's timing he was acknowledging the specialness of this ability, but we never tested Hogahn's knowledge in any way. As a scientist, Sheldrake did test the ability of some of the animals he met. He arranged for the people to return home at randomly selected times, and he tried to eliminate all possible sources of the animal's knowledge other than mental telepathy, such as the distant sound of the person's car coming along the road. The animals always passed these tests. Speed and I were never scientific, and in fact, I actually gave Hogahn as much knowledge as I could about my return: when I left in the morning, I told him in a happy tone that I'd be home early, or in a sad tone that this would be a long day. My focus when we were together was always on our connection. I would never have thought of trying to trick him.

I think that I understand Hogahn's awareness. Most of the time in our relationship I stayed connected to Hogahn. I stayed aware of his awareness. And he of course stayed connected to me. He knew that I was aware.

At school, however, I closed off my part of our connection. Like the people in the business meeting, I focused exclusively on getting things done. Of course, I continued to feel things from moment to moment, but these feelings were rarely connected to Hogahn. I blocked my awareness of him while I was at work.

The instant I made the decision to go home, however, I opened myself to all my feelings. I wanted to be home. I wanted to be with Hogahn. On different days, I might feel longing, or fear that something had happened while I was away, or happiness at the thought of seeing him. I would think about stopping for groceries on the way home and reject the idea because I just wanted to get home to him. But always, a half hour before reaching home, I was strongly connected to him. I was a bundle of emotional energies reaching out to him.

When I reconnected, Hogahn sensed it. I suspect that the people whom Sheldrake studied, and the many other people whose animals know they are coming home, have a similar pattern of disconnection and reconnection. At the job they block their feelings. When they start for home, they release these feelings and their animals, who have stayed connected, respond.

Sheldrake's mental telepathy is empathic awareness that travels over larger-than-usual spaces. It is touch at a distance.

Animals are essentially and continuously connected. And this is why we are not hurt by them. We do not experience their rejection, their shutting out of our core self. Animals do not hurt us because they stay connected to us.

Living with Hogahn taught me the absolute seriousness of staying connected. Someday, some moment when we are resting in a calm, sunlit world, a danger could enter, and our lives could depend upon keeping ourselves open to the energy around us. Then, in facing the danger, our lives could depend upon keeping the connection with the other members of our pack.

And Hogahn taught me that this attunement which is part of bodily survival is lovingly entwined with the attunement of spiritual connectedness. Staying connected means continual, beautiful awareness of the changing, flowing universe. It means absorbing, adjusting, transmuting the energies, until we are in harmony with each other and the world. Staying connected is being at one with the universe.

DISSOLVING BOUNDARIES

I circle around
I circle around
The boundaries of the earth;
Wearing my long winged feathers as I fly
Wearing my long winged feathers as I fly
I circle around
I circle around
The boundaries of the earth.

NATIVE AMERICAN CHANT

BIRDS come to us as ordinary-world, physical birds, and they come to us as visions. Sometimes, they come as messengers from the spiritual world. Birds have a special ability to help us cross the thresholds between different worlds.

We cannot grow without crossings. One of the first crossings, the bridge of birth, is a time of great peril for the infant. She is crossing from the safety of the womb to all of the dangers on the outside. It is the moment of breathing on her own.

Birth begins the lifelong flow of separation and connection, feeling the self as a single center and feeling the self as part of the whole. It is the beginning of awareness of self and other, and the beginning of the need in each of us to find the harmony of the whole.

Crossings combine the double promise of growth and disintegration. Any change from one state of being to another holds within itself the potential for not making it to the other side: getting trapped, getting overwhelmed, losing the soul. In the face of this ultimate danger, one of our stories gives the job of delivering the human infant to a large bird. A stork carries the baby across the threshold. We trust a bird to complete the crossing.

During my childhood illness I dreamt repeatedly of crossings. I had one recurrent dream in which I had to cross a small footbridge from one island to another. I *had* to cross; there was no question of staying where I was. Both islands were safe; the danger was being on the bridge. I don't know whether I was crossing from sickness to health, or life to death; it was probably both. Health and death were both new islands where I would be peaceful and free.

In another dream, I was a bird and simply flew away. I flew from my fourth-floor bedroom window over the small blue fishpond in the courtyard of our

apartment house in New York. I circled the courtyard, a safe, enclosed space, looking down on the
garden, the water, the tiny fish. The walls of the
apartment houses were the walls of a canyon, and
above me the sky was a protecting dome. My breath
and my body were in perfect harmony with the air
which circled me. In the air, I was myself again, alive
and whole and at one with the universe. I was a bird
of dissolving boundaries.

I think all of us, especially as children, connect
to birds in this elemental, bodily way. All of us know
how to fly. We know how to be a bird—wings
spread, body light, gliding and soaring over the land.
We know this vision. In dreaming visions, you *are* a
bird. You cross the threshold between the worlds
and you are free.

I have met men who have given up the emotional world. They are hard-core: at the core is the
densest mass of resistance, so that nothing can make
a connection. There is no space to tie a rope.

These men do not allow feelings that could
bring about a need for another creature. Connection
is a form of dependence, and they are afraid to depend. But sometimes they are able to connect to
birds. They don't think of birds as building nests and
having babies. They watch large, solitary birds,
hawks and eagles. You can see them, sometimes,
with a parrot on their shoulder. They are not imi-
tating Long John Silver—he is just a manifestation
of *them*. They and their parrots are trapped tempo-

rarily on the ground, but they know how to fly and one day, they will soar again.

This freedom, so powerful in the emotional realm, is preciously tenuous in the bodily world. We all feel the vulnerability of a bird in our hand. The bird who flies over the land, into realms of the spirit, is also a physical creature with perfect wings. We know, directly in our body, both the strength and fragility of these wings. We may not think about it, but our bodies understand, because we have a spinal cord, and other cords, that are incredibly reliable and strong but can break in one instant and change our lives forever.

When we hold a bird in our hand, we hold the cord between life and death.

I was sixteen when I first held a bird in my arms. It was summer, and I was a counselor at a camp in the Laurentian Mountains of Canada, walking with Cob in the forest. Cob was of some unknown age, unmarried, the kind of man who spends winters in a snowbound cabin with only his dog. I was in love with him, and it was a privilege to be alone with him that morning.

We were walking in the deep cool shade of a pine forest when there was a great commotion above us. We couldn't see, but Cob said that an animal must have gotten into a nest. There were shrieks and flappings, and two baby owls drifted down to the needles at our feet. Cob picked them up, one in each arm.

The parents were in the treetops flying back and

forth frantically. The tree trunks were straight and round as telephone poles but much higher. After watching the pattern of the parents for a while, we finally spotted the nest.

"I'm taking them up," Cob said, "one at a time." And he handed me the second owl.

He placed the first baby inside his flannel shirt and started climbing. At first I watched him. But I didn't see him reach the top or place the baby into the nest. I was absorbed by the bird in my arms.

The owl was fairly big already, almost ready to fly. It was not afraid of me. This was its first experience out of the nest, and it was fearful, but not of me. It huddled against my chest as if we were back in the nest and I were another owl.

When I felt it pressing into my chest I instinctively quieted my breathing and we grew calm together. I cooed to it in low owl tones. Cob returned to find the owl nestled in my arms. He watched us a while and then took it up to its higher nest. The owl and I were together for less than an hour, but it would be the last time for a while that I would feel that kind of connection.

When Dana and I returned from camp at the end of August we found my mother lying in the middle of our parents' bed, her arms like dry cornstalks at her sides. She was too weak to meet us at the door. She was so thin and silent, I thought at first it wasn't her. She died in February.

I spent that winter, before and after her death, at the ocean. There were still public buses running to a few of the city beaches each morning. The people on the bus had been working in the city all night, and were returning, exhausted, to the small beach houses which they rented cheaply during the winter. They slept through the long ride to the ocean. I was the only person awake and looking for the water.

No one noticed me and I looked at no one. I returned each afternoon by three o'clock to be home for Dana. On the days when I showed up at school, Mondays and sometimes Tuesdays, I brought "please excuse" notes which I carefully crafted in my father's handwriting. No one questioned me. When I wrote the notes, I pretended I was my father, feeling my hand as his hand. It was easy for me.

The boardwalk, the hot dog stands and penny arcades, were boarded up for the winter. The shacks formed a ghost town, and the ghosts were the only presences in my life who acknowledged my mother's dying. The beach itself was accepting, but not warm and comforting like the desert. It sheltered its silent creatures under the sand, in the crevices of the rocks, in the beams of the boardwalk. We were ghosts at a ghost beach, foggy, barely tangible. We huddled in shells and feathers against the stinging Atlantic wind. It was not a time for talking or making friends. The winter ocean, with its reliable waves, pounded me into staying connected.

Otherwise, although spring came and then summer, I moved in the fog of that winter beach, huddled and out of touch. It was only after Soren's birth, eight years later, that I felt again that essential clarity at the core of the self.

Like the baby owl in my arms, Soren assumed that I knew what to do. He was so alive, so connected to everything, that he dragged me back to awareness. He moved to the lapping of the waves and the drumbeat of the rain. He sniffed whatever the dog sniffed and he licked the cat. He watched birds as if he were practicing maneuvers. When he was still very young we met a large bird together, and the fear that had held me since my mother's death was transcended.

We were in the desert hills of northern Mexico, the same desert that gave me the rabbit and its leap. Although he was already walking, Soren still liked to go for long rides on my back. He rode strapped in a black shawl that crisscrossed over my chest and around my waist. My legs were strong and I moved with the freedom of a dancer over the ground. We walked all day, exploring the world.

There was a small village a few hours from home where I liked to get soup and tortillas in the marketplace. The soup was delicious and the ground was swept clean. I put Soren down to play with the other children while I ate lunch. After several trips we established a destination, a rock set into the eastern slope of one of the hills beyond the village.

The rock bent inward at its center, creating a hammock of stone made fuzzy by tiny lichen. From the hammock we could see down into a deep valley and up to the faces of the surrounding hills. We would go to the rock and play for a while in the immense stillness, watching small birds landing and taking off from nearby bushes. When the sun had reached halfway between a point directly above and the point at which it would disappear behind the far hill, we would leave for home.

One day while lying on the rock I saw a movement in the bushes directly to my right. It was a large movement accompanied by rustling noises and I was startled. Then everything was quiet. I got up and approached cautiously. As I got closer, I noticed a line of smooth brown earth through the bushes. There was no animal, only its path, into the valley. I started to step onto the path and a vague sense of fear came over me. I felt a chill at my back. I looked over at Soren. He was not on my back. It suddenly occurred to me that he was part of me now, and that my courage came from our connection. It was an interesting discovery. It could have worked the other way, after all: a baby on your back could make you more cautious, more afraid to explore.

I thought of getting Soren and descending, but the sun was approaching that halfway point which meant that we had to start for home. On the way back I calculated how we could manage enough time to go into the valley.

The best plan would have been to sleep overnight in the village and start up the hill in the early morning. But there did not seem any easy way to arrange sleeping over in the village. There was no inn. The people who lived there did not have extra rooms, extra beds, extra anything.

So one morning when dawn was just barely beginning in the eastern hills, I dressed Soren and myself warmly, wrapped him on my back, and headed for the village. I walked steadily and more purposefully than usual. We did not stop to look at birds and flowers. It was still early when we got to the village.

I nursed Soren and ate a bowl of corn soup. I bought an orange and a bag of crackers, which I wrapped in a second shawl tied below Soren at my waist. Then we set out for the rock.

I had to check the shape of the opposite hill and the pattern of the bushes to be sure it was the same rock. We had arrived so much earlier than usual that the rock was still in the shadow of the eastern hill. I walked past the rock to the beginning of the path and stopped. It seemed like such an enormous thing, this descent. I looked back at the rock. Shadows wiped out its inner hammock of lichen, making it hard and rejecting. I turned and we started down.

There was definitely a trail made by animals, and perhaps also by people who came to gather plants. The trail zigzagged down the incline, level and easy for a short while, then steep and rocky. When it began to get dangerous I sat down and carefully lowered myself from rock to rock. Soren's weight became very evident then, as the motion of sitting and shifting my body forward had to be coordinated with the motion of his body on my back. Like a horse and rider, I would say "hold on" and he would grip my shoulders and keep his weight centered as we leaned precariously. After a few times he did this by himself as soon as our balance seemed in danger. I still said "hold on," in response to his motion, but now it was no longer a command.

I concentrated upon the ground, watching the shape and texture of each rock and the pattern of successive rocks passing under my hands and feet. It was only when we stopped to rest that I let myself look around and down. Then contours and bulges of light and dark started to grow out of the far ground, like flowers emerging at sunrise in a garden. Patches of dark became the green oval bulbs of cactus plants, and lighter patches grew into the yellow points of ground flowers. A winding streak turned into multiple lines of light brown and circles of gray, a riverbed.

As we got deeper the path began to flatten, the earth became soft and comfortable, and my steps were easy. We were entering the heart of the valley.

The ground was covered with tiny succulent plants growing amid small stones and some sand. The yellow flowers were everywhere, like buttercups. The cacti grew like small trees with fat bulbs; the older bulbs were dark green and the youngest were almost yellow. There were two things we could not see from above: that the bulbs contained white flowers, and that there was a small stream of water in the center of the riverbed. Everything was warm and peaceful.

I put Soren down on the soft sand and he began

playing with the grains. I lay down to rest along the edge of the riverbed in the shade of a flower bush. The air was quiet and we both fell asleep.

When I woke up Soren was lying by my side with his head on my shawl, still sleeping. I watched him for a while. Then I carefully disentangled my shawl from my shoulders and stood up. He moved slightly, as if to acknowledge my motion, and then sank back into sleep.

I sat down on a stone a little away from him and took off my shoes. The sand seemed to be breathing slightly under my feet. I got up and started moving. It seemed that as I stepped the earth inhaled, rising with its own breath to meet my feet. Its steady motion lifted me off the ground so that I floated gently from step to step. I began to dance.

I danced in a large circle over the breathing sand. My whole body felt light and quiet, as if I were a cloud that was floating across the space, bobbing with the same rhythm as the wind through the air and the water over the ground, so that we all turned together in a perfect dance.

Afterward I lay down next to Soren and waited for him to wake up. I didn't want to wake him. But the sun was well over the place that I thought was the halfway point, although I couldn't be sure because I was seeing the cliff from below now, a very different angle. I rolled over so that the side of my body touched his. He stirred. I waited for him to wake, slowly, and then he nursed for a long time. I didn't rush him. But when he was finished I tied him onto my back quickly. We had a long way to go and the sun was already low. I knew now that I had miscalculated the sun because of the unfamiliar angle.

We climbed strongly for the first hour. The sun was hovering just above the hill line when the bird appeared. It was close to dusk, when small animals come out of the rocks and crevices of the steep hills and large birds watch for their movement. We had already seen several chipmunks scurrying behind rocks ahead and behind.

The bird came from high above, somewhere out of the rocks at the very top of the western hill. It hovered over the valley, watching. Even at that great distance it looked large.

Although Soren was behind me, I could tell from the tension in his legs that he too was watching. He held himself centered and straightly alert on my back.

I tried to climb faster but soon realized that this was impossible. We were on the steep higher part of the climb, where I had to step carefully and deliberately from rock to rock, using my hands to balance and pull us from one level to the next. It was simply not possible to move more quickly.

The bird circled the valley with enormous grace. I leaned against a rock to rest. It was clear that we would not make it to the top before the sun went down behind the western hill. But there would still be at least an hour of indirect light before actual darkness. And then, if we were lucky, there would be a moon. I tried not to worry.

Soren moved suddenly. I looked up in time to see the bird swooping down along the opposite hill and then circle, very slowly and steadily, along the face of the hills at their height. I pressed Soren against a rock and faced out toward the valley. The bird's wingspan was longer than my height. The sense of its power was incredible. It turned toward me. It kept its eyes locked on us.

I was gripped by fear. The bird was large enough to carry Soren away if it could get to him. Of course, I would not let it; it would have to kill me first. But the bird possessed all the power of its claws and beak in the air, and we were at our most powerless on the side of the cliff, balanced precariously. I pushed Soren tighter into the rock and dug my feet into the sliding ground.

The bird passed enormously before us. Its great wings caused a stream of air to flow across our faces and a rushing sound to echo through the valley. Then it was past, soaring again to the top of the hills. It circled around.

I climbed again. If we could reach the flat ground at the top of the hill we would be out of danger. I climbed, keeping my eyes carefully divided between my hands and feet on the surface of the rocks and the position of the bird. Soren kept his weight perfectly balanced.

Again, Soren noticed it first. I felt his legs tighten, and when I looked up, the bird was descending. Very deliberately, I picked up two palm-sized stones, holding them lightly in each hand. I wedged Soren between two protruding rocks and braced my sides against their hardness. Facing out with Soren behind me, I waited. At the core of myself I was perfectly calm. I knew that whatever happened I had to protect Soren, and I knew I would do this.

The bird seemed to expand as it approached our level. It was a magnificent bird. It made you want to take off with it, to circle, soar, descend with it, over the world. It turned toward us, following the contour of the hill. It looked into our eyes.

Then, all of a sudden, I recognized it. It was like recognizing the face of a person who is important to you, but you are not sure why; like recognizing the body of a person you have been with, but it is uncertain when. It is the sense of recognition that is important.

As the bird soared Soren and I climbed. As it descended we rested and watched it. When it soared we climbed again. We climbed effortlessly. I had become almost weightless, fitting the structure of my body and Soren's into connection with the structure of each rock to keep our balance; the effort of pulling our weight from one rock to another was gone. Soren too was weightless, like a warm feather on my back. It was dusk now. The bird gave us its energy and protection.

Birds come to many of us as spiritual guardians and protectors. Peter Moeau, a Maori spiritual teacher, told me about his first awareness of fantail birds as his protectors. He was fourteen years old and driving very fast on a country road, his grandmother beside him. He saw three fantails and with his attention focused on the birds, he slowed down the car. Around the next bend a boulder had fallen onto the road. If he had not slowed down, the car would have crashed into the boulder, probably killing his grandmother and himself.

After this event he knew that the fantails were his spiritual guides. They came to him at moments of stress and crisis. But sometimes they came at ordinary moments and he was not sure of their message. He asked his grandmother how he could know what they were telling him.

"You will know," she said. "But if you don't know, it is because you are trying to put it into words; you are worrying about it. They are just there for you, and you don't have to know why."

This understanding, coming across generations and continents from Peter's grandmother, was an important insight for me. I have felt the significance of birds all my life, but I have never received a message in words. When I try to derive a verbal message from meetings with birds, I become confused and know that the words are wrong. Peter's grandmother let me know that birds simply come to me and that their presence is enough.

Peter's deep connection to birds brought me another insight. On his visit to Kauai he was asked to do healings, and he allowed me to be present on one of these occasions. He was working with an older man who was not well. With his own strong arms holding the weight, Peter opened the man's thin arms to either side. As their arms opened, Peter felt both of them spreading their wings. He was giving to the man his own feeling of opening his center, touching the unknown. He was giving the man the feeling of freedom.

A few days later, as I was thinking about this healing, a strong, clear image from the past returned. I saw Soren, a year or two old and balanced on my hip, stretching one arm as far as he could into the space to his side, raising it between the plane of the ground and the apex of the sky. He spread his arm, elbow straight, palm up, reaching. Whenever he did this I felt my awareness increase and focus. I felt that something significant was happening.

You have probably seen small children reach and stretch in this way. When you see a child doing this, you become attentive. You look up, and sometimes you see only space, the sky or the ceiling, and sometimes you see a bird. You can see a bird twice. You can see a bird in the wingspan of the child's arm, and you can see a bird in the direction of the reach.

Birds are everywhere in our visions because we are part-birds. We feel our body as the body of a bird. And we feel the rhythm of freedom as the rhythm of flying.

After the meeting with the large bird in the canyon, many boundaries dissolved. I was seeing clearly, and the owls who had drifted down from their nest in the forest when I was sixteen returned to me. They came back in a dream, as spiritbirds.

I was walking on a winding path through the site of an ancient temple, like a Mayan temple at Palenque in Mexico. I climbed a hill and entered a structure. The first floor was dark and cool, cavelike. I saw a stair and climbed up. I was standing on a large, open floor, with no walls or roof, four columns rising from the ground marking the corners. There were two enormous birds, about the height of NBA players, waiting for me. They were owls, with long winged feathers and deep wide eyes. One of them took me against its chest, and the other opened its wings partway, enough to surround me. They held me in their wings, surrounding me with radiant light and ecstatic feathers.

5

POWER

WHEN we sit on the back of a horse, her powerful body is an extension of our own body. When she gallops across the land, we are moving with her as one unified power, horse and rider.

Humans have a close, complex connection to horses. We think of horses as both tame and wild, creatures with the power to save our lives and the power to kill us. Horses live with us, not in the house, not in the wilderness, but in a transitional space.

Human houses are too small for horses and too rigid for humans who do not fit. Rejected by human society, Mary goes to a stable to deliver the son of God. When humans hurt us, we find safety with the horses in the barn.

The dwellings that we build for horses are extensions of our own dwellings. We place the stables behind our house, away from the road which connects us to town and our human culture. When we want to get away from our public life, we go to the privacy of our house. When we want to get away from the house, we go to the stables.

In the building of dwellings, as well as in human relationships, we tend to follow familiar models. So we re-create parts of our own house—the roof, floor and walls, and the separate stalls, the gates and boundaries—in building stables. And we re-create another human structure, the power structure, inside the stables. We exert our power over the horses.

The story I am about to tell you caused me to rethink a whole set of ideas about strength and power. I had worked with these concepts for years in human relationships, but somehow, in the context of horses, I saw them with new clarity. Animals can do this for us. When Stormy Weather came to Eleanor, both of their lives changed. There is an echo in their story, a symmetry of beginning and end, that is especially moving. In delving into the rhythms of their connection, I feel that I have just touched the surface; the meanings continue to unfold.

Eleanor is a tall, stately woman, with the look of bodily strength you get from growing up in the country and working with horses. I met her at the pool where we both were swimming through the New England winter. We spoke to each other in those conversations that occur in locker rooms where everyone is feeling good because they are stretching and relaxing their bodies, but I don't think we ever talked about animals. The winter had been both long and severe, and like everyone else at the pool, we discussed the weather and how we couldn't wait to be swimming outdoors.

At the end of May it was still cold, we were still swimming indoors, and I mentioned that I would be leaving next winter to work on a book about human-animal relationships. Her eyes widened, and she told me about Stormy Weather.

Eleanor was born in the desert of Texas, grew up in the farmlands of central Florida, and spent her teenage years in the hills of Maine. Her father was a Texas horseman, and whenever the family moved, it was always to a place where her father could keep his horse. The family house and the stables were just different parts of her home to Eleanor. From the beginning she rode tucked in front of her father on his horse.

The situation was difficult for Eleanor's mother, who was afraid of horses. She imagined all of the accidents that can happen around horses happening to her child. In her mother's visions, Eleanor wandered into the corral and was kicked by a horse. Or she was riding with her father and as the horse reared, her father lost his hold on her and she fell and was trampled. Her fears were compounded by her knowledge that there was something wrong with Eleanor's sight. The horse was already much more powerful than her tiny child. The horse would sense the child's added weakness and use it against the child.

Eleanor was born with limited depth perception. Depth perception is the ability to see into the
distance, beyond the space immediately around us.
It also enables us to see that one thing is closer to us
than another. Those of us with normal depth perception rarely think about this visual connection to
our world. It is only when we make a mistake that
we become aware of its importance.

When Eleanor walked, she couldn't see the
ground clearly. In normal perception, you can see a
change in the surface of the ground before you step
forward: you can see when the sand becomes water
at the rim of a lake, or when the rock above becomes
the rock below at the edge of a cliff. The visual systems of almost all living creatures are designed to
see edges. We are tuned to any change in the surface: the boundary between ledge and gorge, between floor and stairwell. This visual perception of
a boundary in everyday life means that there is a
difference in depth, a difference in closeness to us,
between the two surfaces. It protects us from falling
off cliffs or down stairs, and it gives us our visual
experience of a spacially deep and wide, three-
dimensional world.

Seeing an edge is also the way all of us see each
other. When you see a brown snake coiled around
a brown branch, you are perceiving tiny differences
at the edges of the snake that give you its shape.
Gestalt psychologists say that you are seeing the figure, the snake, against the ground. This is how you
see any shape, predator or prey. A fox and a hawk

can see the tiniest difference at the edge between a white rabbit and the white snow. And animals have a natural camouflage against being spotted by having a bodily surface—fur, scales, feathers—that blurs their edges, making their shape blend as unobtrusively as possible with the mottled ground beneath them.

So Eleanor, as a three-year-old child, did not see the edge and fell down a staircase. She was fitted for glasses after this fall. But it is hard for a child to keep her glasses on. Essentially, her visual world was a sphere of clarity close around her, and a blur beyond this sphere. It was like walking perpetually through a light fog.

Still, Eleanor's father took her out to the stables and with him on his horse. And her mother could see that Eleanor was happiest around horses. So with real courage, she took Eleanor to a neighboring ranch for riding lessons. Soon Eleanor was riding and learning to show horses, but almost always within the corral. They were living in Florida now, surrounded by fields of wild grass and flowers, with trails that led into rich green hills. But when Eleanor was allowed on the trail, it was always with a group, never just she and the horse wandering together. She was mainly kept safely within the boundaries of the corral.

And then one Sunday, her father said it was time for Eleanor to have her own horse. They went out looking, and Eleanor found Stormy Weather.

Stormy was young, two and a half, and almost

completely untrained. He was white with a dark gray mane that had not been groomed and was rough and disheveled. He had deep bruise marks on his chest from barbed wire. He had grown up as a rodeo horse, been beaten, terrorized, and finally sold. He was gentle if you approached him on the ground, but he wouldn't let anyone on his back.

Stormy was being sold for two hundred and fifty dollars. Eleanor wanted him. She didn't know why. Her father kept saying that she could have a better horse, meaning one that was much more expensive and trained, but Eleanor held her ground. They brought Stormy home.

This was the beginning of a relationship that would last throughout Stormy's life, and which, as Eleanor speaks now, you can tell is still there at her core. Stormy threw everyone who tried to get on his back: first Eleanor's father, then a professional trainer whom her father hired, and lastly Eleanor. After a few weeks the trainer, who was an honest person, told Eleanor's father that he was wasting his money and that the best idea was to leave the girl and the horse alone to work it out. Perhaps he sensed the connection between the horse and the girl. It was good advice, because soon Stormy allowed Eleanor to sit on his back. "Gradually," she said, "he began to accept my commands."

Eleanor took the word "commands" from the horseman's language. But it seemed out of place in their relationship, and I was about to question her when she sensed what I was thinking.

"People in the horse world see the relationship as one of dominance and submission," she explained. "The rider is taught that if he doesn't dominate the horse, he will be dominated." She said that she has been in the dominant position with many horses over the years, horses she has trained and shown for other people. Like most horsepeople, she does not reject this basic framework. She just knows that it was not this way with Stormy Weather.

Stormy simply decided to trust her. She knew something, nonverbal and indefinable, when she first saw him, and at some point he knew it too.

Stormy and Eleanor went into the green hills together, both of them feeling for the first time the joy of wandering. It was an incredible accomplishment for Eleanor to be out of the corral and on her own. There had always been people watching the ground for her, paving the way. There had always been fences, enclosed spaces where the ground was level and known, boundaries of safety and of limitation. There were gates to make sure she didn't stumble and fall.

But a child needs to explore. A child wants to discover things about the ground that are unexpected. A child needs to roam a little in order to grow. And so does a horse.

Stormy and Eleanor could leave in the morning and wander all day in the Florida hillsides. He saw the ground clearly and didn't stumble. They were safe with each other.

Florida has many low-bending trees, with

snakes who wind themselves casually around the hanging branches and through the cool, smooth leaves. Like any horse, Stormy shied away from snakes. Eleanor could not see the snakes, some of them poisonous, from which Stormy saved her. They hung from the branches over the path, out of the range of her depth perception. When Stormy sensed a snake, through seeing or smelling, he would leap almost sideways off the path. He was very careful not to rear or make any motion that might cause Eleanor to fall off his back.

When Eleanor was a young teenager, the family moved to north-central Maine, where the houses are widely separated from each other by woods and farmlands. Being with Stormy helped her to make friends during that transitional time. They would ride into town to the square where the teenagers hung out. She was confident and relaxed because Stormy was with her, and Stormy was friendly and calm around her friends. But he never let anyone except Eleanor onto his back.

One beautiful fall day her father tried to ride Stormy. Stormy threw him over and over. Eleanor told me this with a smile and a heightened energy in her voice and body. I got a sense of her deep affection for both of them, and her pure joy as she re-created the scene in her mind. I must have been looking at her intensely, responding to her energy, because she looked down, paused, and then said:

"My father was good at everything. He was better than me at whatever he did, and he let me know it. So I guess I really liked what happened. Stormy was the only thing I did better than him."

I thought about the intertwining relationships: her father, her mother, Eleanor, and Stormy Weather. If Stormy was Eleanor's closest companion, her mother and father might have sometimes felt sad that her connection to Stormy was stronger in some ways than her connection to them.

One evening Eleanor's mother said: "I think if there was a fire you would save that horse before anyone else in the family." Eleanor remembers that she said this with an edge of jealousy.

And any of us might have felt jealousy, in addition to longing for the closeness of Eleanor and Stormy's relationship. They were connected to each other empathically.

In most of our relationships we move in and out of empathic connection. Sometimes we are truly tuned into each other, and sometimes we feel we have to struggle—dominate or be dominated. We weave a rhythm of opening and closing ourselves to each other, seeing and not-seeing, being there and being absent.

Eleanor and Stormy were really there for each other, tuned in and responding. They gained inner strength from the safety of their connection. They gave their strength to each other. When things changed dramatically, they responded together to the change.

Eleanor knew that something was wrong. Stormy had always loved to go out riding. He began to hesitate now, to slow down, as they were leaving the pasture. He tripped over a stone on the path. One day, he stopped at the gate.

Eleanor knew; asking the vet to look at him was just a formality. Stormy's sight was going.

They had a dog, Trevor, and the horse and dog liked each other a lot. Eleanor began to take Trevor out on the trail with them. With Trevor along, Stormy relaxed more. The dog stayed close to the horse, guiding him. They went slowly and not so far.

When Stormy's sight grew worse, Eleanor rode him only within the pasture, where he knew every piece of the ground by smell and touch. She rode him just as much as he wanted, letting him feel safe with her as he had let her feel safe with him. She invented ways they could ride together without making him leave familiar ground.

She showed me an old film, which her father had converted to videotape for her, of Stormy and Trevor playing together in the pasture. The dog was lying on the ground alongside a simple wood-rail fence, and Stormy was standing close by him. Trevor stretched his neck through the fence and nudged Stormy's nose with his nose. Stormy waited a minute, and then initiated the same nudging of noses with Trevor. They repeated this gentle game over and over, I don't know how long because the film segment ended. I wished I could have seen more.

Stormy's last months were painful; the injuries he suffered in the rodeo had damaged internal organs. He died in his stall when he was thirteen, not old for a horse.

Only a few weeks after talking to Eleanor I met Kendra, a woman whose life had also been changed by a connection to horses. The odd thing was not the similarity of Kendra and Eleanor, but the similarity of Kendra and Stormy Weather. The woman and the horse had both been beaten by a human who needed to dominate and control. Both had been saved by a human-animal connection.

Kendra had been married to a man who got angry unpredictably and who, when she was unable to diffuse his anger, hit her. She lived in constant fear and, at the time of the beatings, terror. Like many of us, she could not talk about her fear and the things that happened with her husband. She could not talk of these things to other people in part because other people did not want to know.

Kendra lived near a stable which raised and boarded horses, and she started going there on walks. She had a camera and liked to take pictures of the horses. Later, she became a professional photographer of thoroughbreds. But at this time she just hung around the stables because she felt better there.

When she was frightened, she went to the stables. After she was beaten, she would walk down to the stables, open one of the horses' stalls, and huddle there in a corner. She felt safer in the stall; she felt, in some way, that the horse would protect her. Being there with the horse, she told me, she gradually began to pick up the horse's strength. Eventually, the sense of protection and strength she received from being with the horses enabled her to leave her husband.

She did not mention riding, or galloping, or even grooming the horses. She may have done these things, but the central experience for her was the gathering of strength. It was an essence she picked up and absorbed and collected within herself by sitting in the stalls. She took into herself the horses' power. This strength enabled her to do something we know is one of the most difficult things for anyone to do: To end a relationship in which, locked and entangled together, are love, commitment, and terrifying abuse.

I thought about these horses, Stormy and the others—powerful animals who give to humans a sense of power. And I thought of Stormy and other powerful horses whom humans abuse. It is not only weaker creatures who are abused: the framework of power in human culture seems to generate abuse wherever it goes. Eleanor said of this framework, "You dominate or else you are dominated."

Eleanor's words echoed in my mind. I have witnessed the results of this way of thinking in human relationships. I wanted to understand how it was the same and, I hoped, different in our connections to horses. I was troubled, as I always am, when I think about the pervasiveness of this framework and the damage it has done. I decided to talk to Joannie, Penelope's companion, about this framework. I knew she had been part of the world of horsepeople for many years and understood it.

Joannie and I sat in her garden with mugs of fragrant coffee and talked about horsepeople. She began by telling me that, unlike Eleanor, her father was not a horseman, and she had to struggle to get her first horse. Both of her parents were afraid of horses. They had moved from the city to a farm when their children were young, but they were interested in vegetables, not farm animals, and certainly not horses. Yet Joannie and her sister had a single-minded, unwavering desire to have a horse. They pushed so hard that the parents agreed to let them raise sheep. If they proved with the sheep that they could be responsible for animals, their parents would think about getting a horse.

For four years Joannie and her sister cared for their sheep, showing them at state fairs and selling some of them for feed and the money to buy a horse. They were impeccably responsible. And they remained focused on horses, sometimes riding on the backs of their strongest sheep. When Joannie was thirteen, her parents reluctantly honored their bargain.

The girls were allowed to trade three sheep for a pony. The pony was pregnant at the time, but no one knew this. The sisters read books on how to train horses, but the books never explained why you should do one thing or another. No one in the books had tried to understand how the horse might be thinking or feeling. The girls made many mistakes while trying to train the pony. All of this time she was carrying a baby, which was certainly more important to her than having someone on her back. She bit them, threw them, and delivered a colt the following spring. With the birth of the colt, the girls became horsepeople.

Joannie jokes with her sister and friends now about their obsession with horses. "We think it's genetic," she said. "We say, 'You've got the gene for it,' or 'It's in your son or your daughter.' " Joannie has traced the gene in her family back to two uncles who used to raise and train horses for the Newark Police Department. "It's something that you just have to do," she said. "As long as I can ride a horse, even when I'm very old, even if I'm crippled, I'll ride."

Then she spoke of the danger involved in working with horses. Horses are larger than us, and physically more powerful. Because of its great strength, the horse can hurt and even kill the human.

Experiencing all relationships within the framework of dominance, humans assume that the horse will use its strength against them. The stronger creature will try to dominate. And so humans do whatever they can to be dominant. With whips, barbed wire, and cunning, they compensate for their weakness.

"Most people get control by beating the horse

into submission," Joannie said. Then, as in any relationship, the dominant one must constantly work at retaining his power, keeping the subordinate under control. He has to keep asserting himself, senselessly yelling at, beating, and intimidating the other.

We were simultaneously talking about human-horse and human-human relationships. The elements of abuse echoed back and forth between the levels.

"Everyone is now admitting they're scared to death," Joannie said. "And then they're transmitting the fear to the horse." The fear is always there, under the surface: fear that the horse will throw them or kick them, fear of the loss of power. The horse picks up the human's fear and also becomes afraid. But the human is not open to the horse's fear; he has closed himself off, trying to maintain control. Horse and human are not together in their fear; they have become antagonists, fearing each other.

Joannie's riding companion is a mare named Ginger. When they ride together, Ginger trusts that Joannie knows what she's doing. When they are approaching an external danger, a river or a busy road, Ginger does what Joannie wants because her trust overcomes her fear of the situation. Without this trust, she could bolt or rear, putting both herself and Joannie in danger. When she and Joannie go into the wilderness, away from roads and human dangers, she takes the lead.

We trust another creature who understands that we are afraid to cross the river and who talks to us, touches us, calms us down. If you stay with the horse, talking, grooming, just being there, trust will develop. You and the horse together will be less afraid; you will find ways to calm each other. This is a relationship of mutual trust and respect, mutual empathy.

"We calm each other," Joannie said. "When I'm upset about anything, I go sit with the horses."

A relationship in which there is a struggle over dominance cannot at the same time be safe. It cannot be a space of trust. When one creature exerts power over the other, fear enters the space of the relationship. Fear means that our bodies and our selves are in danger and we act to protect ourselves. We build walls to block emotions; we design war plans, strategies to deceive and outwit. But the danger is not coming from outside the connection. It is within the sanctity of the relational space, inside the connection. This is destructive to the very core of the self, the center that feels the connection. We can never feel safe.

When we exert power over another, we are at the same time closing ourselves off to awareness of our own fear. If we really felt the other's fear, if we let their fear inside ourselves, we would stop the hurting, because endangering the other would be endangering ourselves. It is like Penelope: something wrong for Joannie was something wrong for both of them. In mutual empathy, both creatures feel any fear that is present in the connection.

In trying to understand and explain the complexities of power in human relationships, Jean Baker Miller looked at the concept of power from two different frameworks, *power over* and *power with*. In the prevailing framework, with humans and animals, we live in a culture where we are taught to exert power *over* other beings. We are taught that if we don't take over, we'll lose.

In a framework of mutual empathy power flows between you. When there is real trust in the connection, you give each other strength. When the relational space is a safe space, both of you grow in inner power. Jean Baker Miller calls this *power with*. Eleanor and Joannie rejected the prevailing framework of *power over:* beating the other into submission. They instinctively, and thoughtfully, created relationships of *power with*.

Because horses are so strong physically compared with humans, and because we are often denied the flow of mutual power in our human relationships, we seek out horses for inner strength. Sometimes, in our thinking, horses become less than the complex, real creatures that they are. We begin to think of them as symbols, abstractions of strength.

It is important to remind ourselves that each horse is a living individual, exactly as we are. The primary energy that we pick up from horses may be the sense of power. But when we stay aware, we can feel their many sides.

One night on the island of Vieques off Puerto Rico I witnessed a wonderful ritual of power. Every man on the island who owned or could borrow a horse saddled up at sundown and rode his horse to the village. The men and horses began to gather. The energy was like heat lightning, all over the place, in the ground beneath their hooves, in the air around them. The horses pranced and whinnied, the men shouted and laughed, and those of us watching from the porches and yards were electrified. Power flowed through all of us. Then they took off, all of the men and horses galloping up and down the main street of the village, hooves pounding the ground like a giant drum. You could easily imagine another time, when men and horses went off to war together and the strength and courage of your horse could mean life or death for you.

Afterward everyone talked and played together. There was no parade, no formal structure; we just gathered together, horses, riders, and the people in the village.

I had not thought of this gathering for several years, and when I remembered it at first I thought of the horses as male. But although the riders were men, half of the horses were female. I had seen these horses the day before and the day after, calm and gentle creatures, grazing in the fields that slope down to the island's sea. Half of these horses were mares who gave birth in the stables and raised the island's wonderful colts.

It is so easy for us to fall into human habits of thinking. Power is not male or female, power does not have to be domination, power is not the absence of gentle love. In Hawaiian, power is called "mana." Mana has the sense and feeling of power as it occurs in the animal world. Mana flows through creatures as it flows through the universe. When we are in harmony with the universe, we feel mana. When we gallop with a horse, mana flows through us as one body—horse, rider, wind, earth—the body of the world. Mana is spiritual power. Mana is the power of energy in connection.

Stallions and mares have power, and they have gentleness. Mares and stallions have fear, and they have inner strength. When we reduce any creature to a symbol or sign, we stop connecting to the core of the animal, its self.

When we go to horses because we need strength, we sense that they will share their power with us freely. If we go to them not to dominate or abuse, but to make a connection, they trust and accept us. Then their energy is our energy and our energy is their energy, in mutual empathy.

We find the strength of the horse and we find our own strength as a single feeling. We feel power which is coming from the horse and coming from inside ourselves at the same time. We experience power *with* the animal, not over or against it. The merging of energies, the electricity of connectedness, like the gathering on the island, increases everyone's mana.

Inside us, deep and perhaps buried for a long time, is our own power. At some moment in our lives, even if it was only a moment, we were confident and free. We were once clear about ourselves, felt our centers, felt that we moved in harmony with the world. We have inside us the knowledge of being able to fly, to ride the waves, to leap.

Moving—floating, riding, flying, and leaping— is power. Feeling—feeling the stillness at the center of the self—is power. Harmony—being in balance with the energy of the universe—is power.

When we are with a powerful animal, the animal's energy comes into contact with our own power. Our power is released from whatever walls and gates we built for protection. And when we rediscover our power, we are truly free. We give our strength and happiness lovingly to the animal who has helped us. The animal is energized and gives more power back to us. Power plays and leaps within our connection.

Horses are spiritual beings, and they are bodily creatures with internal injuries and fears, like Stormy Weather. Sometimes we seek them for inner strength, and sometimes they bring us other lessons, other aspects of connection.

"When you're upset and you sit with the

horses, do they give you strength?'' I asked Joannie.

"It's not strength so much as calming," she said. "It's like meditation, a calming effect." And I thought of the jackrabbit who taught me meditation. Joannie's teacher was a horse.

When you learn to be with horses, riding them and caring for them, you are training your own body to be physically strong. You develop muscles to wrap your legs around a horse. You are also training your mind to focus, to be aware, to tune into the connection between you and the horse and between both of you as a single unit and your surroundings. You are all there, together, in the present moment. You learn a form of meditation, a meditation with you and the horse in motion. With the growing physical strength comes an inner calmness. It is a calmness of body and soul.

And with this strength and calmness, you have a sense of inner freedom. You are free from whatever it was that used to block you—tension, fear, confusion about yourself. You feel the energy, and you are free.

Stormy was strong for Eleanor, but only because he was able to trust her, allowing her on his back. Being able to trust has at least two meanings here. He was able to trust because Eleanor was trustworthy; she would not harm him. And he was able to trust because he had the inner strength to let down the walls he had built to defend himself against other humans and their abuse. He was strong enough to be gentle and vulnerable.

He saw Eleanor not as just another abusive human, but as she was, someone who brought him love. And then he freely shared his strength with her: his incredible motion, his focused sight, and the energies of his self. He and Eleanor grew together in inner power.

The abuse of one creature by another is as terrible in human-animal connections as it is in human relationships, and the free flow of power is as clear and beautiful. I am hopeful that if we, men and women, can transcend the struggle in our connections with horses, we will be able to transcend it with humans as well.

6

PROTECTION

W**HEN** Soren was leaving for Japan to study carpentry, he asked if Hogahn, who was his dog originally, could live with me. "Of course," I said. "He'll protect me." There had been robberies in the neighborhood recently, and my house in Massachusetts was surrounded by a pond and woods to the north and west, so that someone could easily approach after dark without being seen.

Soren laughed. "Hogahn doesn't exactly bark when someone comes to the door," he said. "If a burglar came, he would probably lick him."

But Hogahn sensed that his connection to me was different from his connection to Soren. Soren, who is strong and relatively fearless, did not need much protection. When Soren was in a hurry, he would lift Hogahn like a small child into the bed of the pickup. I could not lift him. We were just about the same weight, and Hogahn was younger and stronger. As a woman, I faced dangers that Soren and Hogahn did not have to know about. After a week of living with me, Hogahn was barking at anyone who came near the house.

Our protecting relationship began early, with me as the initial protector. Hogahn was a puppy, about seven months old, when Soren left him with me for the first time, only for a weekend. It was a cold, late November morning and the water in the pond was just beginning to freeze. A thin layer of ice held blowing leaves and light branches, but was much too tenuous for animal paws.

I was hanging up the laundry in the backyard on a long clothesline which stretched from the giant oak tree next to the house to the spruce at the edge of the water. A light blue sheet was lifting itself with the wind and was trying to sail off over the pond to join the sky. As I struggled to trap it with a clothespin, Hogahn was panting warm clouds of air at my feet, lifting and dropping a two-foot oak branch that had fallen into his loving possession.

Focused on capturing the sheet so that it draped evenly over the line, I distractedly picked up the stick and tossed it down the hill toward the fence that separated the yard from the water.

I had tossed sticks for him before and knew the approximate distance they would go, depending upon their weight and my motion. This stick, however, caught a gust and, flying where the sheet wanted to go, sailed across the yard, over the fence, and, with a fine skater's touch, glided onto the pond.

As I looked up, I saw Hogahn racing through the gate and, with a magnificent leap, crashing through the ice just short of the stick and into the water.

Time froze as I stood at the clothesline. I thought: Soren has given me this child to watch over. He is my first grandchild. I have to save him. I was penetratingly aware of the dangers of the pond in November. I had fallen through once and saved myself because I had stayed very calm and moved very slowly. I knew that Hogahn could claw at me in his panic, pulling me down, and we could both go under.

The next moment I was standing in the water and Hogahn was swimming toward me, breaking the ice with his front paws. He seemed a little startled by the intrusion of the ice in his path, but definitely in control. I went as far as I could until the pond bottom sank down under my weight and the ice water penetrated my jacket, and I stood and waited. He swam into my neck, and I lifted his puppy-body and carried him out of the water. He seemed to acknowledge that there had been some danger. He stayed quietly in my arms as we went across the yard and into the house, not squirming in his usual way to get free. Inside, I rubbed him for a long time with a towel. Afterward, he went over and examined my wet clothes, which I had thrown in a pile on the floor. He liked the fact that my clothes smelled of the pond, that we both had that swamp smell.

The next protecting event between us occurred

in Vermont about a year later. A group of friends converged on Soren's cabin for the weekend, and I brought my tent, which I set up in the clearing in front of the cabin. That night, after everyone had settled down, Hogahn came and lay down beside the tent door. I hadn't asked him to stay with me, and it was the first night he had not slept inside the cabin. He'd decided on his own to guard me.

It was two years later when Soren brought Hogahn to live with me. At that time in my life I had insomnia. I often had trouble falling asleep, and when I fell asleep easily, I would wake up at two or three in the morning.

Generations ago when the pond was swimmable, my house had been a summer cottage, with two doorless bedrooms at the top of a flight of stairs. Since I lived alone, the open doorways were never a problem.

On Hogahn's first night in Massachusetts I turned down the woodstove, turned off the lights, and kissed him good night. He was stretched out comfortably on the couch when I went upstairs to bed.

I was lying under my down quilt with the radio playing softly when I heard breathing. My eyes were not yet used to the dark, but I saw Hogahn's eyes shining above the foot of my bed. My bed is a piece of foam rubber on the floor. He stood looking down at me.

I lifted myself up on one elbow and ordered him out of the room. I was completely willing to care for him in every way, but I was not willing to make my bad sleeping pattern even worse by having him in my room. He was going to have to sleep downstairs.

I got up and, leading him to the top of the stairs, pointed down. He looked calmly at the staircase and settled himself at the top of it, a few feet from my room. I assumed that a compromise was being negotiated, and I realized that there was no door that I could close. I patted him, told him to stay, and went back to bed.

In about ten minutes he came back into my room, but so quietly that I didn't know until he had flopped down at the bottom of the bed. I took him out again. I wasn't angry, and I didn't want to yell or pretend anger on his first night away from Soren. Perhaps he was lonely. But my voice was firm: I really did not want him in bed with me. He lay down on the landing again, sighing deeply.

I fell asleep. When I woke, several hours later, he was stretched at the foot of the bed. Somehow, in spite of my neurotic sleeping, he had managed to enter the room and lie down on the bed without waking me.

My normal pattern when I woke in the middle of the night was to stay awake for several hours. I daydreamed, listened to all-night talk shows, heard the New York news. I was an expert on the latest subway murders in Manhattan.

I felt him with my toes. It is very cold in my house on winter nights. When I close down the woodstove for the night, the coals burn slowly, staying alive for morning. During the night, however, the stove cannot radiate heat, and the house temperature drops dramatically. By four in the morning it is 40 to 50 degrees, depending on the outside air and the strength of the wind. In a real cold spell, I have to get up in the middle of the night to feed the stove in order to keep the pipes from freezing.

So when I pushed the soles of my feet against Hogahn's body, the warmth felt good. It vibrated up my legs and into my stomach. I lay there trying to decide what to do. I was torn between happiness in the moment and predictions of future sleepless catastrophes. If I didn't make him leave right then I would certainly lose my authority over the situation. But I didn't want him to leave the room at that moment. I was awake and his presence was good. I crawled down under the quilt and emerged at the other end of the bed. It was still dark and I couldn't see his face, but I put my head next to his front legs and rubbed his stomach. He sighed. I woke up in the morning with Hogahn's back pressed tightly against mine.

From that moment I was free of insomnia. I slept peacefully with Hogahn every night. When I woke in the middle of the night, I patted him and went back to sleep.

When Soren returned from Japan two years later he took Hogahn back to Vermont. Hogahn was Soren's dog, and besides, I was moving to Kauai, where dogs must be quarantined for the first four months after they arrive. After he left, I watched with an odd sense of detachment to see if the insomnia would return. It never did. Hogahn had given me the pattern of safe sleep, and the pattern stayed with me even after his physical presence was gone.

Don Juan says:

> I don't have any personal history. One day I found out that personal history was no longer necessary for me and, like drinking, I dropped it.

I dropped insomnia. There is a widespread belief in our society that if you have once been an alcoholic, you are always an alcoholic, always addicted to some pattern of thinking and acting—that each day is a renewed struggle to stay free of the past. If you think this way, the part of you that is addicted is always with you. But it doesn't have to be. You can really shed that part of you; you have that power. It is a question of how you think and feel about the pattern. You are walking on a path and you can leave that part of you behind, letting it dissolve in the rich earth along the way.

Hogahn let me feel safe and comfortable with sleeping. When I had fully experienced this new pattern, I could shed forever the old pattern of fear.

Many people sleep with animals. A friend of mine, a writer in New York, sleeps with two very large, powerful Great Danes on an ordinary double bed. One afternoon I was exhausted and lay down to rest. The two dogs decided to take a nap with me and leapt gracefully onto the bed. After we had all settled down, I was squeezed tightly between one of the Danes and the wall. I couldn't move in any direction except up. I fell asleep and woke up feeling happy.

Dogs and other pack animals sleep tight against each other. In the colder climates and winter seasons this brings natural warmth. Even in the summer the temperature drops at night and a little warmth is welcome.

One spring, when my back was not good, I went to rest at my friend Douglas's house on City Island, New York. Joanna, who was also living at the house, had just adopted two puppies, Muky and Sasha. Because of my back, I spent most of my time on the floor with the puppies.

I watched Muky and Sasha flop down next to each other and next to me day and night. Their motion was incredibly accurate. They circled, dropped, and landed exactly at the boundary of the other creature. They landed touching the boundary—not on top, not with any separation, but just exactly meeting the other in a firm connection.

For safety, back touching back is the perfect position. Each of you can cover the two halves of the space, the front and back entrances. You are free to jump up if there is danger because no one is on top of you. If danger comes, the one who senses it first will instantaneously communicate it to the other through the bodily connection. You won't have to whisper, call across the room, or even worse, get up and go into another room to warn the others. When you think about human houses, with the bedrooms spread out horizontally and vertically, the arrangement is the worst possible one for the pack's safety. In fires, the parents are often unable to get to the children to save their lives.

I have thought about why it is so comforting to sleep with an animal. An easy answer is that Hogahn was just a substitute for a human, with the implication that if I were psychologically more normal I would have found a man to sleep with me. But this answer is wrong, and in its facile dismissal of the animal, it misses some important insights about animals, humans, and the ways in which we feel safe and happy.

During sleep we are tuned to a rhythm that is very peaceful and healing. People who study sleep say that the brain renews itself through this time of calm.

In dreaming, we are tuned to rhythms that are mostly internal. We create the rhythms of dream experiences within ourselves, and tune into a level of reality that is far away from ordinary waking experience.

In order to safely and calmly go to this other level, we need to be able to relax about the ordinary waking level. We do not have to tune it out completely; we know that it is there, and when the alarm clock rings we can be aware of the sound as part of our dream, or as part of ordinary reality. We have that choice. We straddle both levels.

But to be soundly asleep, we want to be able to

feel secure about the ordinary world, which is the place our body resides. We need to know that our body is safe while we focus on our mind. We need to know that when we go off to a new level, we can safely leave our body lying on its bed.

Animals are the guardians of our body, our bodyguards. They have perfected the ability to sense the dangers or disturbances of the ordinary world while in the state of sleeping. They have, more accurately than we, a double awareness.

Also, more than we, they can separate sounds or smells that can be safely ignored from signs of danger. In the middle of the night, when the window is banging from a high wind, the dog hears it and rolls calmly back to sleep. But when a living creature is making some noise outside, even the smallest noise, the dog is instantly alert. His whole body tells us that we had better pay attention. My house in Massachusetts was very old, and there were noises all night long. There were mice in the walls, squirrels and acorns on the roof in the fall, baby birds in the eaves in the spring, and always, coming over the pond, the western wind. Hogahn distinguished between noises that I could ignore and noises that I had to hear.

From his days as a puppy, Hogahn had stayed with Soren at various construction sites in northern Vermont. For both of them, inside and outside were not separated. The sona tubes rose first like new trees. The foundation, once poured and dry, lay like the clearing, windblown with needles and leaves. When the roof went up, there were still only two-by-fours, wide open on the sides, and both of them treated the space as a canopy of trees, shelter from sun and rain. They walked under the shelter without thinking of walls.

Even when the walls were actually up, plasterboard stuck onto the studs, they kept most of the link between inner and outer. The windows and doors were always the last to be put in, perhaps because they were ordered from faraway companies and never arrived on schedule. Without a tangible threshold board, or stairs that would complete a path to the door, they romped in and out of the house space freely, leaping the height from whatever angle felt good. Watching Soren finally place the last door on its hinges, I remember Hogahn's look, the feeling that we had ruined the entrance to our pack's den. We had put up this obstacle, this rigid boundary, that dogs couldn't move through and even humans had to struggle with, groping for knobs and keys. We had not only ruined the ease of passage, we had jeopardized the pack's safety, dulling the smells and sounds that flowed from the outside to warn of approaching danger, and making the inside a trap if we needed to escape quickly.

But he accepted the door as he accepted everything about the human world, graciously, uncomplainingly, fitting into our customs. He was my bodyguard, even when I made it difficult for him, even when I stupidly put both of our lives in danger.

At home with Hogahn in Massachusetts, I watched him smell everything, and in a genuine effort to increase my awareness, I tried to smell what he was smelling. After he had sniffed a stick for a while, I would pick it up, inhale, focus, inhale, and find I smelled nothing. But my efforts were not a complete failure. There was one thing that I learned to smell, and that was Hogahn himself. It wasn't that I didn't smell him before. It was that after a while I distinguished many of the subtle molecules of his smell, floating in harmony. After a while, I loved his smell.

If you put your head down on his body, your nose just hovering beneath the fur-tips, you could get a good understanding of the air around him. Its scents brushed over his fur and clung to it, much as they do with a woolen sweater, settling in the spaces.

In the winter months he smelled of the woodstove smoke, even in the middle of the night when the logs had long burned down to smokeless coals. He carried the smoke smell from evening to morning.

His winter smell was also of snow, clear and cold even when he was inside and it wasn't snowing. The snow molecules circled around the smoke molecules.

His spring-autumn smell consisted of variations on a swamp smell. When the pond wasn't frozen, Hogahn waded and fished in the water three or four times a day. People came to the house and were overwhelmed by this smell. Polite people might compare the smell to that of a cranberry bog, making the observation as if they were narrating a nature film, distancing themselves from any personal sensation. Then they would move to the other side of the room in small increments, trying to make it look like a natural flow, as if the other side of the room were drawing them downhill to settle in a corner. My less polite friends would scream: "He smells like a swamp" and jump to the other side of the room.

I also smelled the pond, the scent of ferns and algae, of misty droplets of water, but it was a wonderful smell to me. It was an ancient smell, amoebas and pond moss. It was the smell of murky waters and fog, the smell of thickness, of all the things you can't see, of all the things you can't hear. And it was given to me, tangible and real, in Hogahn's body. Burying my face in Hogahn's fur, I entered a world where stagnant waters kept unchanged the smell of ancestors.

And then, at a deeper level, there was Hogahn's body. This smell, beneath the winter purity and the summer thickness, was immutable. This smell was warm and sweet.

When Soren was between one and two years old, we lived in a miserable apartment with no washing machine. I let the diapers pile up in the bathroom (disposable diapers had not been invented yet) until the last one was wet; I hated the Laundromat. One day after a long walk in the pure air of winter, we entered the diaper-pungent, overheated air of our windowless bathroom. Soren, who was barely talking at that time, said very clearly: "Horsey." He recognized the stables.

Young children, not yet trained to find fault, enjoy all kinds of smells. Soren and Hogahn both loved horses. They would have let the diapers pile up for another week. Of course, an intelligent animal would have found the idea of saving and washing diapers ridiculous anyway. She would have found the whole concept of putting diapers on her child absurd.

As soon as the water was bearable for me, Hogahn and I swam at Lake Chauncey. We were in the water as it was warming and stayed until the leaves were falling around our floating hair. Dogs were not allowed at the public beach, so we walked from the boat launch to a cove used mostly by fishermen and animals. The path went along a ridge bordering the lake, with forest trees on the lake side and a cornfield on the other. After the cornfield there was a forest where hunting was allowed in season. The whole area was state land and was as close to wilderness as you can find in central Massachusetts.

The area was unpredictable, at least to me.

Sometimes there were fishermen trolling close to the shore and people with dogs walking the trails, and sometimes it was deserted. The only times I could predict the presence of people were summer weekends, when the place was almost crowded, and hunting season in the fall.

I learned many lessons about danger from Hogahn, and many of them came from Chauncey. We were in nature there, in Hogahn's territory. He was the leader, the wise one.

Once hunting season started, there were often gunshots coming from the forest beyond the cove. The hunters were supposed to fire only within the forest, never around the boat launch or the cove. But some of these humans were not hunters; they were drunken men with loaded rifles in their hands. They wore bright orange vests and a few shot each other dead every year.

One day we were swimming at Chauncey when the gunshots started. Hogahn tensed immediately, got out of the water, and pointed to the trail back to the truck. I was nervous also, but my rational mind was saying, It's all right, the hunters are in the forest, we're safe here. I was going to ignore the sounds and stay. But Hogahn was so nervous and insistent that we left, although much less quickly than he wanted. I was thinking that we were really safe because of the rules, and that I was only leaving for Hogahn's sake.

This experience was repeated several times. I left when the shots began, not because I was listen-

ing to my own instinct, but because Hogahn was so
upset. The sounds were making me nervous, but I
let thoughts about the rules of society overweigh my
feeling.

Then one day we were alone at the cove, happy
in the water, when the shots started. Hogahn ran for
the shore and I followed him, taking some time to
gather my clothes and shoes, and as I was stupidly
standing at the edge of the lake, a bullet went by
me. I ran to Hogahn, who was at the head of the
trail. Another shot came, and this time I was able to
locate the sound, and it was coming from the cornfield, the direction of the trail that took us back to
our truck.

I saw that our best chance of escaping was along
the lake, where we would be at the bottom of the
ridge and the shooter would be at the top. If he
wasn't aiming at us, but just randomly firing across
the cornfield, the bullets would go over our heads.
If he was aiming at us, the shots had a good chance
of hitting one of the trees before it got to us.

I called Hogahn and pointed to the forest. He
came immediately and we started through the
woods at the edge of the lake. There had been a trail
once, but it had long ago been returned to the forest.
Although Hogahn could travel much faster than I,
he paced himself to stay close to me. He stopped,
turned, and waited as I awkwardly climbed over
rocks and branches. The bullets kept coming. From
a distance, Hogahn looks much like a deer. And
since drunken and stupid hunters have shot human

beings because they thought the people were deer, it is very likely that the shooter was aiming at Hogahn or me, or both of us.

We made it to the boat-launch parking lot and into the truck. In the cab of the truck, catching our breath, we hugged each other. I drove soberly home.

We continued to swim at Chauncey, and there were many days when we were all alone, or when our only companions were herons and fishermen. But at the first sound of gunshots I was out of there. Hogahn did not have to wait for me anymore. I understood that if a sound, a smell, anything, gives you a feeling of danger, you must honor that feeling.

Society has all sorts of rules and expectations which may tell you that you are safe. But if you don't feel safe, you aren't. You cannot count on human social structures; people break the rules all the time. You can count on your own feelings, and the instinct of your animal companion. He is listening to his body, and to the connection of his body to the body of the earth. He knows the vibrations of danger.

One beautiful spring day we were walking along the cornfield on our way back from the cove. Hogahn was ahead of me, loping along, examining roots and tree trunks for other dogs' smells, enjoying himself. The cornfield was on our right and on our left was the ridge with the woods sloping down to the lake.

111

It was not unusual for us to see young boys climbing up the slope, especially if they came with bicycles, which they left on the trail.

Suddenly, a man appeared from the woods and stepped onto the path. He was carrying a fishing rod and pail. He stepped onto the path between me and Hogahn. I was initially startled by the man because he had appeared so suddenly, but as soon as I saw the rod and pail, I accepted his presence.

I saw Hogahn come back to me, moving in a wide curve to place himself on the path between me and the man. Hogahn is an extremely friendly dog, and would normally go up and meet a person. The man moved forward on the path at a relatively slow pace. I waited a few minutes, warned by Hogahn's response, and then began walking. On the way back, Hogahn stayed between me and the man. He didn't stop and examine any of his usual spots. He kept the man and me in his awareness.

I thought afterward about the incident, especially the moment when the man stepped onto the path into my sight. He appeared very silently. If someone is climbing the slope from the lake, he normally makes sounds that tell you of his presence.

I have a vivid image of the man at that first moment: he is looking down the path, in Hogahn's direction, so that I can only see the back of his head. And I clearly remember feeling fear. I am not talking about the initial sense of being startled. I mean that looking at the back of the man, his head and shoul-

ders, I felt frightened. Then I saw the rod and pail
and thought, It must be all right.

I think if Hogahn had not been there the man
would have attacked me. He thought there was no
one around who could help me. It was only when
he stepped onto the path that he saw Hogahn. I
picked up the signal of danger and I dismissed it.
Hogahn stayed with it and guarded me.

Once again, I had blocked a feeling of fear. I still
was not acting from the core of myself.

It took patience on Hogahn's part, but he finally
taught me awareness of danger. His final lesson was
intricate and layered. He showed me that he might
not always be able to protect me, that I must act on
my own.

Soren had been away for almost two years, and
the house in Massachusetts was deteriorating in several ways. My neighbors had always helped me with
leaking pipes and blown-away roofing, but there
were so many problems now that I didn't want to
ask them.

Hogahn and I were spending many weekends
in New York, staying at City Island with Muky and
Sasha. On one of these trips, I was sitting in a coffee
shop with a friend when a man she knew joined us.
This man could fix pipes and patch roofs, and
wanted to get away from the city on weekends.

We talked about the possibility of an exchange:

my house on weekends in return for his working on the house. He did not say much, and when he spoke it was only to ask specific questions about the house. In order to answer correctly, I had to focus, visualizing the different parts of the house: the roof was tar paper over the original square cottage but shingles over the newer living room; the pipes were copper in most places but plastic below the kitchen sink. I knew the house intimately, but I had never described its workings to anyone in words. I became engrossed in my description.

Between questions I felt uneasy with him. But there were many explanations for that feeling, and I remained open. After he left, I asked my friend about him. Although she had not seen him for a while, she thought that he was basically a trustworthy person. He had been in computers, had been laid off, and was bitter. But he loved to work on houses and she felt his personal problems would have no effect on our barter arrangement.

When he called me only a few days later, I was surprised. I was back in Massachusetts, washing the dishes in the bathtub because the kitchen sink was not draining. He said that he was coming to Boston on business and he'd like to come over to the house to look at the work that needed to be done. Again I felt uneasy. But I looked at the grime floating in the sink, and I looked at Hogahn, my bodyguard, and I said okay.

When I heard the car pull into the driveway I was in the basement, moving boxes which were blocking the path to the fuse box. Whenever anyone worked on the house with power tools, they blew a fuse, and I wanted to prepare him. Hogahn was outside in the front yard. So the initial meeting between Hogahn and the man, in which Hogahn would have gone over to him as he left his car and sniffed him, took place out of my sight and hearing.

As I reached the front door, Hogahn was pushing against it to be let in, and the man was standing on the path. I opened the door and Hogahn ran in and jumped on the couch. The man entered and sat on a chair opposite the couch. I sat down next to Hogahn.

Again, the man immediately started talking about the house, asking me questions. This time, however, I was in my own house, my territory. I didn't let him take over. I asked him some commonplace, normally unthreatening questions, not because I needed the answers, but to give me a chance to think about him.

How was the drive from New York?

Fine.

Do you come to Boston often?

Once in a while.

Would you like some coffee?

That would be nice.

We were sitting in the central room of the house, the old country kitchen. It is a simple room with nothing of value except the woodstove that keeps us warm. The living room, however, is very different. When I went to get the coffee, he got up and stood in the doorway between the kitchen and living room. He stood sideways, leaning against the doorjamb, partly in the kitchen, looking into the living room.

The living room is an elegant addition to the square cottage; it looks out to the pond with high, wide windows. Two peaceful chairs, an armchair and a rocker, sit by the windows. There is no other furniture. At different times the space has been used as a dance studio and an art studio, and it seems now to be itself when it is relatively empty. But along the walls, holding the energy of the space, are scrolls from China, pottery from Mexico, paintings by Nancy Flanagan, bamboo from Japan. Some of this work is valuable and some is just beautiful, especially in this space. He looked at the room and said nothing.

When I returned with the coffee, he came back also, with perfect timing. Yet I didn't feel a harmony of motions—more a calculation. And then I noticed something. Hogahn was lying at the far end of the couch, absolutely unmoving. When a stranger comes into the house, Hogahn normally gets excited. He paces around, sniffing and exploring the new being, checking things out. Once he is feeling comfortable, he brings the person a ball to play with. Now he lay frozen on the couch, moving only his eyes.

I was already uneasy; I didn't need Hogahn to tell me that something was wrong. But I wasn't seriously upset. This person wanted my house on weekends, and was probably just used to going after whatever he wanted. But I was thinking more in terms of manipulation than danger.

With Hogahn acting so strangely, however, I was now more seriously on guard. I asked the man if he liked dogs. Instead of answering, he began asking me questions about Hogahn: his age, his weight, whether I always let him outside without a leash. Then, while we were talking about him, Hogahn did something he had never done before and has never done since. We were sitting at opposite ends of the couch. He walked toward me, and pushing me with his strong neck and jaw, moved me forward so that he could lie behind me on the couch, putting me between him and the man.

At that point I was no longer feeling nervous or confused; I didn't need any more information. I knew that the man in the house was a danger. I knew clearly and perfectly that I had to act.

I casually looked out the kitchen window, where I could see both of my neighbors' houses. The people next door were gone, but Speed and Enie, who live at the top of the hill, were home. The top of the hill, however, is far away if there is trouble. I decided to pretend that I was going to make the agreement in order to get him to leave.

He asked to see the rest of the house before leaving. Growing up in New York and traveling a lot has made me rather cool when facing danger. I said that I didn't know much about the wiring and plumbing, but my neighbor knew the whole system, and I was going to call Speed to come over and show him around. As soon as I went to the phone, he stood up to stop me. He said that he had to get going, it was a long drive, and he would talk to my neighbor when he came back.

I reassured him that he could have the house the next weekend and he went to the door. Hogahn did not move from the couch. I walked him to the door, acting friendly and stupid, and watched him get into his car and pull out of the driveway. When I was certain that he was gone, I went to hug Hogahn. He came back to life, nuzzling and licking me.

The next morning, I called the man and told him I had changed my mind. For several months I worried that he might show up at the house, but he never returned. Months later my friend told me that she had found out he was taking drugs and couldn't be trusted.

Hogahn had never hesitated to protect me when we were outdoors. We were in his world, a world he understood. I remember when the bullets were flying by us he kept coming back, waiting for me, urging me to hurry. When the man with the fishing rod appeared on the path, he put himself between us.

But in the house, with this man, he was frightened and didn't know how to act. We were in my world, the human world, in which I let this person into the house, served him coffee, talked nicely to him. Hogahn could not attack him, and because of me, it was too late to keep him out of the house.

I will never know what happened outside between them, before I came to the door. But Hogahn was frightened and came to me for protection. It was while we were talking about him that he actually hid behind me. Perhaps he thought that this man, who he sensed would hurt us, was going to live with us in the house as one of the pack. If he was thinking this, he was not so wrong, since I had considered giving this person our house, our den, on weekends.

Whatever Hogahn was thinking, he told me as clearly as possible that I needed to be the protector. He put the problem in my hands, and I acted. I was the bodyguard.

From that afternoon I have listened to my sense of danger: I no longer deny it. I stay aware and I act.

Hogahn taught me, in Don Juan's framework, to be a warrior. In ordinary reality we often block awareness of our feelings. We sense that something is wrong and then push that sense out of awareness. A warrior never blocks her awareness. When another person is about to harm you, that person is generating energy which you can pick up. The other person may be feeling fear, excitement, rage—whatever energy goes with the person's intention to harm. If you have ever been so upset that you wanted to hit another person, you know the kind of energy I mean.

When a warrior picks up this kind of energy, she knows there is danger. In a state of awareness, the energy of the danger is inside her: she stays open to this energy, and her body echoes its vibrations. She feels, with complete awareness, the upsettedness that is within the other and that is now within her, reverberating in the space between them.

This is why Don Juan says that in nonordinary reality, "There are no thoughts involved; there are only certainties." When you are completely aware, the energy inside the other is inside you, and you know what you are feeling. Out of that certainty, you act, in Don Juan's terms, impeccably. When Hogahn leapt into the truck, he was acting impeccably. When Penelope pressed her head against Joannie's leg, she was acting impeccably. They were acting from awareness. Their actions were connected to the energy of the whole, and restored the safety, the harmony, of the whole.

Hogahn taught me that everything matters. He taught me to be aware and he taught me to act on my awareness. Don Juan taught Castaneda to be a warrior. Hogahn's framework was the world of an animal. I think the two frameworks are very close; perhaps they are identical. Hogahn taught me that he would act to protect me, that I would act to protect him, and that each of us would act to protect ourselves. He taught me that these guardianships were all connected and equally important. Hogahn taught me to be a bodyguard. He taught me to be an animal.

7

INNER PEACE

THE connection between fishermen and sea birds has always comforted me. In fishing villages all along the coast I have watched men at the end of a long hard trip throw the chum from the floor of the boat into the mouths of birds. In Maine the receivers are seagulls; in Florida, pelicans. The birds open their beaks and the men toss the chum: fathers putting the worm down the throats of the nesting babies.

It was my second trip to the Homosassa River dock. I had driven down from the Panhandle the day before, getting to the dock in the late afternoon in time to see the fishermen returning from the Gulf. A flock of pelicans waited for their feeding. After the birds had eaten, and the men had unloaded the boats and gone home, I sat with the pelicans in the fading light. It was winter in Florida, and a chilling wind came over the Gulf. We sat there, huddling into feathers or, in my case, a sweatshirt, facing the wind.

I had come to the Homosassa River to swim with the manatees. When the Gulf waters begin to chill, these large, gentle creatures swim into warm river waters until spring. I had planned to rent a canoe to get up the river. But when I got to the dock that evening, the man at the boathouse told me that they only had motorboats. I can handle canoes; I have been using them since childhood. I had only been in motorboats a few times, and I was afraid of them. As a swimmer, I had been almost killed several times by motorboats.

It is motorboats that are the primary killers of manatees. When the manatees come to the surface to breathe, they are hit by the blades. The Homosassa River and several other rivers in Florida are now protected, and there are warning signs all along the way, asking people to slow down and watch for manatees. But a manatee underwater is not visible when you are sitting in the stern of a boat, ten feet or so from the bow and three or so feet above the water. No motorboats at all should be allowed in these manatee waters. People who want to go upriver can paddle or row. The professional fishermen who need motors do not go upriver; they go out to the Gulf.

But motors were not only allowed, they were the only boats available. I didn't know what to do. Watching the fishermen feeding the pelicans comforted me. Sitting with these large, prehistoric-looking birds and watching the sun set comforted me even more. They let me sit right with them, three on one side and two on the other, all of us watching the sun go down. Feeling safe and calm, I decided to go up the river in the morning.

But in the morning light, walking alongside the boats and seeing their size, my fear returned. The boats were wide as well as long—they looked like they were designed to hold several giants with mounds of gear. The guy who ran the boathouse stood next to me, watching me hesitate. I decided to talk to him.

I told him I had come down to see the manatees, and had assumed there would be canoes for rent. I said that I didn't know if I could handle a motorboat. In speaking out loud and feeling connected to another person, my fear came to the surface and I was close to tears.

Instead of acting superior or disgusted, he set about giving me what I needed to get to the manatees. He showed me how to turn the steering rod in the opposite direction of the way you want to go. He gave me detailed directions to the manatees' cove at the head of the river. His voice, and the way he looked directly at me, said he trusted my ability. He helped me relax enough to climb into the boat.

Later, I thought about the way he had related to me, as if he knew me. He had been one of the pelican-feeders the night before. He was still around as the sun was setting, closing up the boathouse and hosing down the dock. He must have seen me with the pelicans. He saw the part of me that he could trust.

I would like to say that I started the motor, steered a plumb line away from the dock, and sailed grandly up the river. It was not exactly that way. I pulled away from the dock and proceeded to go around in a tight, jerky circle. A woman at the rail of her yacht looked down at me with concern. I didn't look back to the dock. I took a deep breath, remembered what the boatman had said, and finally managed a drunken line heading upriver. The woman and I smiled at each other with relief as I zigzagged away.

The ride up the river was amazingly quiet. Set back from the water were houses squeezed in long narrow lots. But the riverbanks were still in a some-what natural state, with rushes growing along the edge and branches of trees hanging over the water. The manatees eat these rushes, chewing great quan-tities and absorbing the juice.

Remembering what the boatman had said, I kept to the right as the river branched. I was now in a narrower channel with no houses. The trees were taller and the rushes thicker and greener. I felt a sound and looked up to see an osprey returning to its nest at the top of a tree.

I was going as slowly as I could now without stalling the motor, and then, around a bend, I saw the cove. It was a widening at the head of the river, with several streams feeding into the space, creating a calm, gentle pond. This was the center of the manatee habitat.

I cut the motor and grabbed a hanging branch to keep the boat steady. I wanted to think for a while about how I was going to approach the pond.

In the boat with me were two small anchors, some rope, my snorkeling stuff, and some food. At that time my back was not good at all; actually, I had a lot of pain. I looked at the anchors. I could lift them, but pulling them back into the boat might not be easy. And then there was the problem of pulling myself back into the boat once I was in the water. It was very possible that I wouldn't be able to do it.

I moved cautiously toward the side of the boat, still clinging to the tree branch, to check the depth of the water. I looked down. Passing underneath the boat, about two feet below me, was something incredible. It was as wide as the boat, gray, with sparkling diamond-shaped lights covering its surface. It kept going as I watched, stretching beneath me its length of ten or twelve feet. I didn't know what I was seeing. It looked like a flying saucer. I had never seen a manatee.

The river was deep and the current strong where I was holding the branch, and I wanted to get to the quiet of the pond. I reluctantly started the motor, keeping it as slow as I could, and putted into the protected cove. The morning sun was warming the western shore, leaving the eastern half in shadow. Since I get cold easily, especially after I swim, I moved the boat into the sunlight. I shut off the motor, and carefully lifting one of the anchors, watched it sink into the water. It was still early, and I was the only person in the cove. I took off my clothes, put on my mask, and dropped off the side of the boat.

The water was dark and murky, and I couldn't see much. I floated quietly, waiting for my eyes to adjust to the water. I began to see shapes. They were gray shapes, large and small, floating underwater. They floated around, passing by each other, shadows in the water.

People who swim with wild creatures, just as people who want to be in the presence of wild animals on land, approach the encounter with respect. They try not to interfere. Of course, this is not really possible. Once you enter the water, your presence affects the other creatures. They notice you; they move closer to take a look or they move away to avoid you. By being there, you are part of their world.

But you can be there with respect and awareness. A rule of swimmers is that you always wait for a creature to seek you out for more contact. If a manatee comes to you, you can swim together. You never force yourself on the creature.

In true awareness, the idea of forcing oneself upon a creature would be impossible. Beings are tuned into each other, and respond precisely to each other's feelings. Don Juan often traveled long distances into the heart of the mountains and into a deeply connected state of the soul to meet an animal

spirit. And then, with the awe that comes from belonging to the immensity of the universe, he waited
until the spirit found him.

So I did not try to get closer to the gray shapes.
They were aware of my presence, and it was their
pond. I floated quietly. I love the water and am
never impatient there. The cove water was comfortably cool, and the sun was warm. I watched little
fish passing around me, feeling as much as seeing
the gray shapes in the distance. In the water, you
are never alone.

And then a young manatee, not a baby but a
child who was old enough to leave his mother's side,
swam up to me. He was just about my length, five
feet, although he was much wider than me—his
head, his round body. He was clearly curious. He
stared at me and I stared back, not purposely, but
because I couldn't look away. I was hypnotized by
his large, dark eyes.

With a graceful motion, he lifted a flipper and
turned to the side. I thought he might be leaving
me. But he circled around me, swimming slowly. I
started to move with him. We circled together.

Then he flipped to the side again and glided toward the center of the pond. I followed carefully. He
turned and waited for me. I am a slow swimmer. He
swam back and forth, probably wondering how any
creature could be so slow.

I realized why the first manatee, the large adult
one, had looked as if he had diamond-shaped lights
covering his back. When the sun hit the water, the

moving ripples created these shapes. The manatee's coat was a hairy dark gray. The diamond shapes were patterns of light bouncing through moving water. When I was between the younger manatee and the sun, he looked the same way.

And then he did something extraordinary. He rolled over so that his belly was toward me. He lay underneath me, his belly a gleaming oval of white. He hovered there. I tried to pat him, but I couldn't reach him. It was just as it is with a dog—he had rolled over, but didn't realize that my arms were too short. So I did what I do with Hogahn: I rubbed his belly with my foot. I treaded with my arms and used my toes to stroke him. He lay there, stretched out, head back, perfectly happy. And so was I.

I finally had to rest; my arms weren't nearly as strong as his flippers. He gave me a last look with his wonderful eyes and swam away. I went back to the boat and in one lifting movement was up and inside it. I didn't even think about it. I wrapped a towel around me, lay down on the seat, and closed my eyes. I fell into a deep sleep.

When I woke there were several boats anchored in the cove. A man called over to me, asking me if I was okay. I reassured and thanked him. I realized I was very hungry, got out my peanut butter and jelly sandwich, and watched the people while I was eating. Three children were in the water splashing around. The adults all stayed in their boats, looking over the side and pointing to a manatee as it swam beneath them. I didn't feel like going back into the water. I was completely exhausted and happy at the same time. I started the motor, lifted the anchor, and steered the boat quite competently downriver to the boathouse.

Of all the animals I have known, I felt the deepest peacefulness from the manatees. They float in perfect synchrony with their world.

Every creature has a rhythm of motion in relation to the water, air, or land. Ground creatures move with little resistance from the air, except in a strong wind, and a lot of resistance from the ground. The air is so yielding around us, it touches us without our awareness. The ground is hard and full of resistance which we need to survive. We depend on the ground to be there, holding us in place. Underwater, or too high in space, we cannot breathe.

Water is both ground and air for its creatures, with powerful resistances of its own. Water is the solidity that keeps its inhabitants stable, and the permeability that lets them breathe. The water is always in motion—streams, currents, eddies, tides. A creature who lives in water is also in motion, with it or against it.

The rhythms of small reef fish and sea cucumbers create two extremes of underwater motion. A small fish darts around in the water, moving in short spurts from one point to another, then resting. During the rest it gathers the energy to spurt out again, breaking through the water. In the resting phase the fish floats with the current, but in the darting phase it outspeeds the water—spurt-rest; spurt-rest—creating a separate rhythm from its surroundings.

At the other extreme is the sea cucumber, who is connected to the rocks, physically and rhythmically. A sea cucumber looks like a rock under the water, dark gray covered with pale white algae. It moves incredibly slowly, clinging tightly to its anchoring solidity. The water washes over it, bathes it, giving it breath. But it, too, has a separate rhythm from the water; its motion is closer to the stillness of a rock.

The manatee moves at the center of these extremes, at one with the rhythm of the water. The manatee floats inside the water. It is not the same floating as a leaf on top of the water, riding the waves; nor is it the same as that of the sea moss attached to the rocks at the bottom of the water, swaying with the current. When you watch the leaf and the sea moss you feel the power of the water and the yielding of leaf and plant. When you watch the manatee, you feel a perfect harmony between the motion of the water and the body of this large, round creature. You feel in the presence of inner peace.

When I was a young woman I lived on Taiwan, where Soren was born. While I was pregnant and after his birth, we took long walks in all directions, stopping to rest in the quiet shade of the island temples. In each temple, we were always greeted by a beautiful statue of the Buddha. We found these statues everywhere, in the tall-columned, golden and crimson temples of the monks and nuns and in the tiny shrines set lovingly by the side of the road. I grew to feel a special calming in the presence of these statues.

The manatees look like Buddhas: substantial and unreal, solid and floating, deep and light. They feel serenely self-contained, and completely connected to everything around them. Swimming with the manatees was swimming in a slow, gentle circle with a pod of Buddhas. When I envision them now, I feel inner peace. They are the Buddha spirit.

There has been only one other animal in my life who has given me this special spirit. Oddly, his soul was the center of two extreme contradictions, an incredible nervousness in certain situations and then, when the trembling had passed, the deepest serenity. He lived with me for fifteen years, his entire life, and so I was given a long time to absorb the many details of his spirit. He was Panda, an Old English sheepdog.

Soren chose Panda from a litter of puppies at the breeder's house, and I remember the man watching intently as Soren made his final choice. I could see that there was something special about this puppy. The breeder said: "This one is very sensitive. Please be gentle with him."

I never had to train Panda. He simply did what I wanted him to do. He followed me around, and if he was playing with Soren and I called, he came immediately. From the very beginning he had a calmness that usually comes with maturity. He lay peacefully watching his world.

Yet he could go into a state of nervousness instantly. Waves breaking close to our feet upset him. When he saw that I was actually going to enter the turbulent water he became frantic. He trembled at loud noises and even mild but unusual sounds. In fact, he trembled at any form of energy that was unexpected.

Panda was less than a year old when my friend Tom and his dog Doc came to stay with us. Doc, who was a mix of rottweiler, shepherd, and perhaps beagle, was older, very aggressive, and immediately dominated Panda. When Doc did not like something Panda was doing, a subtle look would send Panda running behind me for protection. At mealtime Panda waited for Doc to finish eating. Doc lived with us for less than a year, but for the rest of his life, Panda was nervous at mealtime. He gulped down his food, afraid that Doc's spirit was there to take it.

Still, Panda and Doc stayed connected to each other. They guarded the loft together, sleeping back to back. Doc, who had once killed another dog, wrestled gently with Panda. Doc dominated Panda, but it was different from human domination. When a dog has been dominated by an aggressive human, he is terribly, deeply afraid. There is no harmony between the dog and the human. With Doc and Panda there was happiness and harmony. They played and slept peacefully together.

Old English sheepdogs have been bred for centuries to round up stray lambs and keep the herd together. Any being who lived in the house was part of the herd to Panda. He did his best to hold us together.

We were all living at this time in a loft on Chambers Street in lower Manhattan, and although the loft itself was spacious and comfortable, the street outside was crowded with moving vehicles and people, a dangerous place for dogs. We quickly noticed that Doc, in the middle of this danger, did not always respond to Tom's warnings. On the surface, Tom wanted Doc to obey him, to come whenever he called. But underneath, in a place that was deeply embedded, Tom loved Doc's defiance. He wanted Doc to break all the rules. So Doc, responding to Tom's feelings rather than his words, did not come when Tom called him.

Late at night, when all the stores and offices were closed and only a few of the loft dwellers were around, we went down to an empty lot and let the dogs run. But Tom was nervous, knowing that Doc would not necessarily listen to him if something happened. He might sense another dog and take off across the city. So Tom tied a twenty-five-foot rope to his collar, giving himself the chance to catch Doc if he should bolt.

Doc had incredible energy and raced around the

lot like a speed car. Panda floated through life like a fairy-tale sheep. Children called Panda "Cloud Dog." He was white and fuzzy and every child wanted to hug him. He looked much like the dog my grandfather gave me in the hospital. He was slow and steady, and he did his job.

Realizing that he was not going to catch Doc by running, Panda waited until Doc had zoomed past him and then, at just the right moment, grabbed the trailing rope in his teeth. Carefully, he reeled Doc in.

Doc was the alpha dog, yet he let Panda herd him. He let Panda lead him by a rope around his neck.

When Panda herded, he was completely absorbed in his work. The psychologist Karen Horney speaks of this quality of concentration as "wholeheartedness." All of our heart is involved in the action.

If you saw Panda herding, you'd know that he was wholeheartedly there. At the core of himself, he was connected. He was connected to the motions of his own body: watching the path of Doc and the rope, grabbing the rope at a precise point, pulling on the rope with just the right tension and give. He was connected in space to the pattern around him: the shape of the lot, the position of each of us in the herd, the shape of the herd. In all the times he herded, he never came close to tripping Soren, Tom, or me with the rope.

And he was connected to Doc. He did not confront him by jerking on the rope. Once he had the rope securely in his mouth, he ran behind Doc, getting into his rhythm. Then he slowly and gently pulled him in.

That is why Doc allowed himself to be herded. He would never have let a dog lead him on a rope if he'd felt any aggressive or dominating intent. He would have fought the dog and won. But when he was with Panda in the herding mode, he responded in harmony to Panda's gestures. They responded to each other's motions, tuning into each other's rhythms.

Doc was not the only animal who responded to Panda's spirit. One autumn day Panda and I were walking down a country road, listening to the leaves brushing over our legs. Panda was older and had lost some of his sight, but he loved to walk with me, keeping close by my side and smelling the freshness.

We were passing a high metal fence, the kind that costs thousands of dollars, when Panda left my side and floated toward it. All I could see was an empty field next to an aluminum house. A moment later five sheep and two lambs trotted up to the fence. Noses pressed between the diamond wires, the sheep and Panda sniffed each other.

A man came out of the house and stared at us.

"That's amazing," he said. "I put up that fence because killer dogs got to them at night. When they see a dog, they run as fast as they can to the other side of the field."

I wanted to ask him if he would let Panda

through the gate. I wanted to give Panda the chance to herd real sheep just once in his life. But it was clear that the man disliked dogs and strangers, and I reluctantly walked on. Panda came with me as always.

I wish that I had understood Panda's herding more deeply at the time. Throughout Panda's life, we, the herd, would often begin a walk with all of us together. Then, at a busy street corner, we would start to separate—one of us going to school, one of us to work, one of us to the park. Panda would run frantically from one to the other trying to keep us together. Unlike Doc, we ignored him. Sometimes, feeling how upset he was, we talked to him in calming tones, explaining that we had to go to school or to work. But in the end we always separated.

I think that if we had listened to Panda and stayed together, our lives would have been better in some way. We would have a community, a pack, not just emotionally but physically, bodily there. We talked a lot about building a community and then we scattered. We keep in touch; we think about each other. But we are not bodily together; we don't actually touch. I think about Panda and the meaning of herding. In visions now I listen to Panda—all of us listen. The herd is together, circled by Panda.

8

HUNTING

I did not know how much I knew about hunting. I
tried not to think about hunting, and when I did, I
thought of Chauncey. Hunters at the lake had told
me about tracking an animal, putting themselves in
the animal's place, feeling what it was feeling.
Sometimes, when they finally got a clear shot at the
animal, they didn't fire. And sometimes they pulled
the trigger and killed. I think of the person who shot
at Hogahn and me, his finger pushing the trigger
over and over. Did he see that he was shooting at a
woman and a dog?

All animals who eat other animals are hunters.
I knew that, someday, I would have to open myself
to the feelings of hunting. Otherwise, my connection to animals would be partial and ultimately un-
true, letting in the safe feelings and denying the
frightening ones. I would have to face myself as a
hunter.

The first time I really struggled to understand hunting was on a visit to a tiny island that is part of Belize. I was just beginning to learn about reefs, just beginning to open my eyes underwater. I went to the island to visit the barrier reef.

When you look east from the island, instead of a normal ocean horizon you see a gray borderland, almost like a stretch of land but too thin and even, with the whitecaps of waves breaking over the border. This is the barrier reef. Beyond the reef is the Atlantic, with its depths of dangers. Between the reef and the island the water is a shallow, calm green-blue. You can see the sandy bottom, the waving grasses, the translucent green and white fish, from any floating point. Except in a serious storm, the reef protects the channel and then the island from the outside world.

On my first morning on the island I got into a small motorboat with a guide named Lulu and four other visitors, a young couple from Germany and a couple from France. Lulu headed the boat up the channel. After about ten minutes he slowed the motor, curving gently toward the reef, and took out his fishing gear. He baited the hook with a slab of fish and trolled at a steady distance parallel to the reef. I wasn't paying much attention. I was watching the reef.

Then there was a whirl of movement: Lulu pulling fast, the pole bending like a Japanese bow, a beautiful gray fish, about four feet long, leaping back and forth desperately to break free from the hook. Lulu won. The fish lay in the bottom of the boat, very alive, eyes moving and frightened, and Lulu said, "Barracuda." He said it with happiness.

"You eat fish?" he asked each of us in turn, staring into our eyes, his own eyes shining.

Yes, we each nodded. The fish stared.

"Then tonight we will have a barbecue, all of us." And he picked up a club and slammed it down on the barracuda's head. Again he slammed it, and its blood spurted upward, clear red blood, splattering onto the German girl, who was sitting closest, onto her leg and her chest below her throat, a circle of blood like the jewel of a necklace.

She was upset, and using a sophisticated psychological technique, I reached in my gear bag and handed her a tissue. She was upset, not so much at the death of the barracuda as at the battering. Would it have been kinder to let it die slowly from a lack of air? More painful? The people of the island are fish-eaters and Lulu is a hunter. The island people love their world. Of all humans, they are among those who have interfered least with their natural habitat. They respect the ocean, the island, and the reef. When the German girl and I see battering, we see women and children beaten inside their homes. We see war and hatred. Do our feelings have any meaning here, on the island, beside the reef, in Lulu's world? Still, Lulu had battered the fish: it was an event we had witnessed and could not deny.

The girl turned to her boyfriend for comfort and I put on my mask and sank into the water.

I swam away from the boat, seeing the barracuda's face as it was dying, seeing its eyes, and in peripheral vision through my silicone mask the water flowed by. The reef is another world, and I was down there in that world, but I was there with violence and death.

I was winding around through the branches of coral, trying to lose the feeling, trying to let this world be itself. And then, through a passage between two corals, I came into a circle of quiet water, about twelve feet deep and enclosed by coral, and found myself face-to-face with a barracuda. He stared at me unmoving, and I knew, I know right now, that he looked with hatred. I have met many fish in the water. Some are frightened and hide, some are indifferent and continue their nibbling of a tiny plant, and some are curious and even friendly. This one knew whom I had just killed.

He stared me down. I looked away, not knowing what to do, thinking of backing up through the hole I had entered but unable to move. Before I could act, he turned sharply and was gone.

I floated for a long time, breathing with the water. I didn't want to move. At some level, I didn't want to exist. I didn't belong there, in the reef, in the boat, on the island. I felt that in the universe at that moment there was no place for me to be.

In my state of nonexistence, a school of tiny green fish did not notice me. They swam through me, making beautiful green patterns beneath my mask and lightly brushing my skin around my legs and over my arms and chest. Their touch released me and I began to look around.

In the circle very close on my right was a great globe of brain coral, glowing like the setting sun. Attached to this brilliant ball, just slightly behind it, was a fan of purple coral, rocking slowly. And behind the fan, watching me languidly and breathing with the water, was a large green fish with amber stripes and amber eyes. She focused on me easily.

"I'm sorry," I said. "I thought I was coming just to look, but you can never just look. You are part of whatever you enter and everything is connected. Forgive me."

I do not usually give names to wild creatures. When I think of the rabbit in the desert, the manatee in the cove, and the large bird in the canyon, I see their bodies and feel their energy without any names. Our connection is nonverbal and naming seems presumptuous. But perhaps because I confessed to this fish in thought-words, a very human activity, I needed to name her. I named her Amber.

She kept her eyes focused on me, and her attention was enough. She reconnected me to peacefulness.

That night Lulu made a fire and cleaned the dead barracuda, and poached its flesh in coconut milk. He sat at the head of the table and the German girl and I sat next to him on either side. He served us proudly and it tasted incredibly good and we all told him so. Then he carefully unwrapped a piece of tinfoil that he had placed to the side, saving it for the end. "Her eggs," he said, and he distributed them among us. She had been female, and I had met her mate.

Lulu is a hunter. He is clear and aware of the meaning of his acts. He brings food to his family and the rest of the island people, including the tourists, who as guests on the island must also be fed.

Lulu talks to the fish underwater. One day, as I was returning to the boat, he motioned to me to come to where he was floating. I looked down and on the ocean floor, about ten feet below us, was a manta ray. Lulu led me around to the front of the creature so that we were facing its eyes.

"Is it safe?" I asked nervously.

"If it attacks, it will be with its tail," he said, pointing.

I reluctantly pulled my attention away from its eyes. Its body was a star-shaped black mat about five feet across with a very straight, serrated tail. The fluid movement of its body contrasted sharply with the rigidity of its tail. I would have been too frightened to stay if Lulu had not been with me. He talked to the creature, letting it know we would not harm it. It was absolutely clear that Lulu was not into capturing, torturing, or destroying in any way. He killed for food. The manta ray connected to Lulu as Amber had connected to me.

When I bought the house in Massachusetts the oil burner was very old, and it collapsed after the first winter. Not having the money to replace it, Soren and I heated the house with the woodstove for many years.

We bought logs in four-foot lengths and Soren cut and split them. The first person up in the morning and home in the afternoon had to get the stove going. Patience was required, and gentleness: the fire is coaxed into growing strong and giving out warmth. We became aware of the intensity of the cold around us, the difference between a 20- and 30-degree night, and the number and thickness of the logs needed to keep each fire alive through the night. We knew the difference between being three feet or ten feet from the fire, and we arranged our acts accordingly.

The cold was not our enemy; we didn't hate it or try to attack it. We lived with it by being aware. It had its place in the house, like the fire, the dog, and the humans.

When Soren left home and I couldn't handle the wood myself, I got a new oil burner. I didn't have to sense the cold any longer; my thermostat kept the surrounding air almost evenly lukewarm. I didn't have to talk to the fire to keep it alive. The cold and the fire were around someplace, in the basement, outside the walls, and now outside of my awareness.

This is the heart of the matter between Lulu, the barracuda, and me. The barracuda and Lulu are clear about their connection. When Lulu eats a creature he does it with full awareness. When I eat a creature, I have not entered a life-and-death relationship with that creature. Someone else, with patience and even gentleness, raised and fed that creature, or hunted it, carefully stalking. And someone else killed it. The creature, like the cold in my house now, is not a presence for me, and I do not talk to it, either to thank it or to ask forgiveness. It is inside me without my awareness.

The next time I tried to understand hunting, I was standing with a friend, Mackey, beside the Hanapepe River on Kauai. In the unsettled energy following a storm, we were watching the water tumble over the crossing where a few days ago there had been a road and now there were chunks of concrete overturned in the water, with trees and plants from upriver already forming the beginning of a new dam. We were talking about someone we knew.

"He looks at the crowd," Mackey said, while his eyes moved over the water, "and senses who is weak. He goes for them. Like a hunter, he preys on the weak."

A documentary jumped into my mind. Two tigers are watching a herd of antelopes from the cover of bushes, waiting: for an elder who cannot run as fast, for a baby who gets separated from the herd.

Mackey was giving me another chance to understand hunting.

"Is there any other way to hunt," I asked, "besides preying on the weak?"

"When an animal is going for food, it goes for the weak," Mackey said. "When it's going for pride, it goes for the strong."

I now saw a wolf pack, and I was the female alpha wolf. I would fight whenever necessary to retain my leadership of the pack. I was going for the strong. I had never thought in exactly this way before. The old concepts of hunting were dissolving, and I was recognizing the feeling of hunting.

When an animal is seriously hungry, it is close to the crossing between life and death. If it does not eat, it will be weak and vulnerable to other hunters. If hunger goes too far, if the animal is too weak even to get food, it dies. It reaches for anything that will keep it connected to this world.

When your soul is hungry, you are fighting to hold on to the center of your self. There is an echo of that same life-or-death feeling. Emotional hunger can also mean life and death. Human babies left in institutional cribs and given plenty of food nourishment have died from lack of touch and emotional connection.

Food hunger and emotional hunger are very close in the feeling at the core of the self. I am not talking about specific sensations of hunger and thirst, longing and desire, because these are sometimes present and sometimes not. When a creature has not eaten for a long time, the actual sensation of hunger, the desire for food, disappears. But once food is eaten, everything feels better. This is true of emotional hunger; the sensation of need can disappear after one has been seriously hurt. We may feel numb, we may feel nothing. But even in the feeling of nothingness, in depression, we know that inside the self "something is wrong."

Perhaps the most general feeling at the core of the self in any form of hunger is simply the awareness that something is wrong. Something is wrong inside you rather than in the surrounding world. Something inside is out of balance, out of touch. You reach for energy outside of the self that can bring back the sense of being alive, the sense of being connected to things outside of the self that make you feel. You reach for connection.

Why do we go for the weak when we feel that something inside us is wrong? Because we are not feeling inner strength and power; we are feeling some form of weakness. We tune into the weakness in others out of our own weakness. Animals and humans are superb detectors of weakness. In a condition of weakness, we are unable to tune into strength.

We all know, of course, of relationships which seem to be connections between a strong and a weak person. But this strong-weak connection is only on the surface. The person who acts as if he is strong is acting from a deep fear. He needs to dominate and control the other because he is afraid. Controlling the other is a matter of survival. The other is part of his self, intimately connected, and therefore needs to be controlled just as the self needs to be controlled. Controlling the other is self-survival. In this kind of relationship, both are acting from weakness.

Yet when Kendra went to the stables, beaten and emotionally devastated, she was still able to pick up strength from the horse. How was this possible? How, from an inner despair, could she tune into inner power?

I think that the horse, in this case, responded to Kendra's devastation. The horse knew, from a lifetime of training by humans, the feeling of being beaten. The horse, at its core strong and proud, was also a prisoner of the human power structure. It was locked in a stall, fenced in with kindness, but still fenced. Kendra could not have gone to a wild horse in the mountains and made that connection. In a wild horse, Kendra would have found only a strength which she could not echo. In the horse in the stables, she found an echo of her own devastation *and* an echo of the strength and courage to overcome. She found in the horse a complex understanding born from the experience of being broken and retaining, in spite of this, the self's inner strength.

Hunting for pride, as Mackey explained it, is hunting with inner aliveness, with power, with a sense of freedom. Oddly, Hogahn at Chauncey had shown me the difference between hunting for food and hunting for pride, but I needed a few more years to absorb the lesson.

When Hogahn and I first went to Chauncey together, he spent all of his time in high-energy motion. He would chase a stick, play with children and other dogs, sniff the beach, swim with me. His energy was like the sun sparkling on the water.

One summer day, however, he just stopped moving. The air was especially hot and the great sun hung directly over our heads. Hogahn was standing in the water, absolutely motionless, staring down. I had never seen him so unmoving. I thought maybe he had sunstroke.

His motionless staring on subsequent days worried me. When I threw a stick he ignored it. When fishermen came down to the cove he briefly looked up and then stared down again. The only things that distracted him were happy young children and exuberant dogs.

I had recently changed his heartworm medication, and I got out the long list of side effects that they stick in the box. I don't like to give animals medicine; if pills are affecting them badly in any way, it is difficult for them to tell us. But heartworm had killed a dog I knew, and it was widespread in our area. I read the list of side effects, and one of the things listed was depression. Could Hogahn be depressed? I really did consider it. Of course, it didn't make any sense: he was only motionless in the water at Chauncey; on the way to and from the lake, and at home, he was his normal joyful self.

After a few days of worrying about sunstroke and depression, I followed Hogahn into the water. I stood very still and looked down. In a few minutes I saw fish, tiny minnows and larger baby fish. Hogahn was following them with his eyes. Then I saw what he was doing. He was waiting patiently, tracking a fish as it darted around and toward him. When it looked like it was moving into the right position just below his mouth, he lunged. He was fishing.

I had never seen a dog fish. And because he didn't lunge often, but only when he had a good chance of grasping the fish, I hadn't seen this motion. I had only seen the waiting, the patient focusing, on the prey.

Once I recovered from my stupidity, I loved to watch Hogahn fish. I loved his deep concentration, his complete absorption in the hunt. His neck was arched so that he could see clearly into the water and strike quickly down. I saw the great strength of the muscles tightening along the arc of his neck. Once I knew how to see, I saw his mana.

Hogahn's fishing attracted attention from fishermen, who felt a kinship with him. Like me, most of them had never seen a dog fishing. I could feel their excitement as they watched him focusing, tracking, stalking the prey.

But none of us had ever seen him catch a fish.

One day, one of the guys brought over a small fish, still quite alive, which he had caught with a pole. He put the fish in a bucket of water and called Hogahn over.

"Get him," he said.

Hogahn looked down at the fish in the bucket and looked away. The guy was watching Hogahn with excitement. He really wanted to see him attack the fish. He repeated "Get him," with increasing tension, partially growling. Hogahn twisted his neck around to avoid eye contact with the guy and looked out over the peaceful lake.

I looked down at the fish to see if it was moving: sometimes an animal will only go after a creature who is in motion. If a prey is motionless—frozen or dead—the animal will not hunt it. But the fish was moving inside the bucket, and I had seen Hogahn watching it move before he turned away.

The guy then had another idea. He thought that perhaps Hogahn needed to be in the water in order to fish, so he picked up the bucket and placed it in the lake so that the lake water was about two inches below the bucket's rim. He called Hogahn over. Hogahn walked into the water and looked down again at the captured fish. He walked away.

Hogahn knew very well the difference between a fish in a bucket and fish in the lake, a dog on a chain and a dog running free. He wasn't hungry; he wasn't fishing for survival. He was fishing for pride.

Although I have now watched him fishing over several summers, I have never seen him with a fish in his mouth. It is possible that when he gets a fish, like some human fishermen, he lets it go.

All of us who live on the land move in a rhythm of alternating stability and instability over the ground. To take a step, we lift a foot, balancing a little less stably for a moment before we place it down again, returning to stability. A magnificent cougar, leaping from rock to rock, is less stable in the air than when she has her four paws on the ground. She puts the weight of her body into the space ahead and risks falling if her landing is not perfectly balanced. If her muscles and paws are not perfectly coordinated with the distance and shape of the approaching rock, she risks bone fracture and lameness. We all move in and out of stability as we leave and return to the land.

Reaching is a quieter version of leaping. We lean over, putting our weight off-center. First we are centered, then we reach out, and then we return to center.

Picture an amoeba moving through a puddle of water. It puts out a pseudopod, extending part of its body into the forward space. Then it slowly transfers all of its body into the pseudopod, creating a new center in the new space. This is the essence of animal motion. The transition part, between the two centers, is the dangerous part.

In all motion—reaching, stepping, leaping—living creatures move off-center and then re-center in a new place. Inner growth is the motion of the self going through this process. We move off balance to center ourselves in a new awareness.

Emotionally, in the motion of the self, we tune into another's energy, entering another's inner world. The other person's energy is mixing with ours and we are momentarily off-center, unstable. The new element has to find a place inside us.

Hunting for pride can also be understood as hunting for inner growth. It is looking over the pack and selecting the creature you sense will help you with an inner reach, an inner leap. Your connection is the space where you take the risk.

There is a wild dog who lives deep in the Hanapepe Valley. From the moment I saw him I was drawn to the mystery of his center. I call him Darth Vader. I selected him for something I needed to reach.

Darth Vader moves with grace and power over the ground. His large, black body is in excellent shape and he clearly eats well. As soon as I moved into the valley he checked me out, and when I started leaving bones on the back porch he took them.

I checked him out too. He is wild, but unlike the wild goats and pigs who live in the valley, Darth Vader once lived with humans. He has experienced the human world. I think this is why I named him.

Whenever I saw him, I would go to the door or the window and talk to him. He looked away. He refused to acknowledge my presence as relevant in any way. If I took a step toward him, he disappeared.

He showed no fear of me in any of the usual ways. The word that best describes the feeling I picked up from him is "disdain." I was human, and humans are dangerous. But since I was not threatening him in any way, I was a weak human, and he dismissed me.

I watched the wild cats who also come to my back porch. Sometimes a group of cats would be eating some combination of leftover rice and vegetables when Darth Vader showed up. He never chased them; he barely acknowledged their presence. He simply walked up calmly and they backed away from the food. He sniffed it, ate whatever he wanted, and walked away. The cats did not run from him; they did not even hide behind nearby boxes. He had no intention of harming them. I even had the sense that he would protect them if a larger danger, a human, threatened. But they quietly gave him whatever he wanted.

It was clear that I was not going to be able to connect with him in any of the usual ways. And something within me told me that it was important that I make this connection. I was hunting Darth Vader for inner growth.

I decided to practice transmutation on Darth Vader. I learned transmutation from Kahu, a Maori spiritual teacher who, like Peter, visited Kauai. I had asked Kahu what to do with feelings of hostility that I picked up from others. I did not want to close them out; all of my training, professional and spiritual, has been to let feelings inside myself in order to understand them. As a psychologist, I need to stay connected to others even in their most difficult feelings. I have practiced staying connected to feelings of depression and despair. I asked Kahu specifically about hostility because I was sensing it, or something like it, in my personal life and I was having trouble with it.

Kahu said that in transmutation you let the feeling inside and then very consciously, with full awareness, send it throughout your body. You absorb it into your body and your body harmonizes with it. It becomes part of you, part of your whole. When you are there with it, in harmony, it is no longer negative, no longer alien; it is you.

Darth Vader trots up to the back porch. I spot him through the window where I am working; actually, I am able to sense his presence nearing the house before I look up. I go to the back door and stand like a tree in the doorway. He sends me energy that I would ordinarily feel as negative—hostility, disdain.

I let him be. He gracefully eats the rice, egg, and kidney bean mixture. I don't try talking to him anymore. I stay in the doorway, transmuting.

This continues over a period of a few months. He comes and goes in a pattern that I do not understand, so that sometimes I see him twice in one day and sometimes I do not see him for several weeks. But each time, I absorb his energy.

And over time I feel a new quality of energy from him. It comes as a living coal from beneath gray ashes of hostility and disdain. It is the energy of fear. I am human, and he has been hurt by humans. Underneath it all, he is afraid.

I respect his fear. It is something I understand well, and it brings us together. I do nothing to change our ordinary-world relationship. He does not want me to protect him. He does not want to protect me. He doesn't want touching or living together. His way of life is alone.

But we are connected now in another way. I hunted his center, his soul, to understand hostility. He let me stay in the doorway; he let me hang around. He gave me the chance to be with hostility in a safe, calm way. As I transmuted it, I saw that at its core it was fear.

We are cool now with each other. Sometimes he looks at me, right into my eyes. He is no longer afraid of me, personally, only of the human structures which I am part of. Like the cats, I keep my distance, not from fear but from respect. I am not separated from hostility, at least not from his hostility, anymore; it is part of me, transmuted, an element of the whole.

In my kitchen in the Hanapepe Valley there lives a cane spider. It is large and looks like a tarantula without hair. Unlike the other spiders in the house, it does not build webs and wait patiently in a corner of the ceiling. It is nocturnal and fast and scuttles around the floor of my kitchen after dark.

One night I came home and found the spider attached to an enormous cockroach, one of the kind that fly. They were leaning against the dishwashing bottle next to the sink, vertical and embracing. Visually, they seemed to be making love.

I turned on the light, feeling as if I was intruding on a very private act. The spider, who was used to me and knew that at least in the past I had never been a danger, looked at me without moving. I couldn't tell if the cockroach was still alive, but I knew that they were not making love. They were in a death grip. I turned off the light and went to bed, closing with unusual care my bedroom door. In the morning I found the remains of the cockroach, shell and dust, lying next to the bottle.

My house, the valley, the world are all hunting grounds. Hunting goes on every moment all around me, whether I acknowledge it or not. I still struggle to understand hunting. I am seeing it better now, around and within me.

9

ACCEPTANCE

WHEN Eileen was ten, her mother died of cancer. My mother also died of cancer, when I was sixteen. Their deaths were similar, slow and full of awareness. Both women lived with their dying for about half a year, with fear, pain, and a struggle for acceptance. Both left children who needed, as adults, to make some sense of their mother's experience. But there was one great difference in the two stories: Eileen's mother, Anna, had a dog as a guide and companion, a German shepherd named Kirby.

Eileen first spoke to me when she was in college studying to become a doctor. She wanted to work on a cure for cancer. One of Eileen's professors had assigned a reading by Elisabeth Kübler-Ross, a psychiatrist who worked closely with cancer patients and writes with great insight about the process of dying. Eileen had been unable to finish the reading.

At ten, Eileen was very close to her mother, and

highly tuned to Anna's feelings. When she came home from school every day, she knew as soon as she entered the house if her mother was suffering or peaceful. Her mother lay on the sofa and Kirby normally lay on the floor next to the window. If Anna was peaceful, Kirby came to the door to greet Eileen. If Anna was suffering, he stayed in the room with her, letting Eileen come to him. Toward the end of her life, Kirby stayed next to Anna on the sofa. As Anna worsened, Kirby closed the distance between them.

At ten, Eileen was open to the world around her, and experienced emotions with clarity and acceptance. She tuned into feelings, her own and others', and didn't block things out. But no one ever talked to her about Anna's dying. Her father was unable to face death himself, and her brother tried bravely to follow his father's example of silence. Through most of Anna's illness, Eileen and Kirby were in the same state of awareness: they knew what was happening, but they never put it into words.

This nonverbal state was natural for Kirby, his way of being. But for Eileen, who as an adult was studying anatomy and reading psychology, it wasn't working. She had fragments of memories: images of Anna walking across the field, Anna lying on the sofa, Anna leaning against Kirby. She felt the shape of Anna's body, the curve of her breasts and stomach. She stored the smells of the air that winter of her mother's dying, of soups and pies Anna had made while she was still strongly alive; and then, when Anna got very sick, of the confused mixing of these smells with the smells of medicines and pain. Eileen needed to fit these images and feelings into the structure of language. She needed to tell the story of her mother's dying.

I remembered, as I listened to her, that I had needed to tell this story also. At sixteen, I had more verbal memories than Eileen, but my family had also been unable to talk to me. I remember one night I was coming home from the hospital, where my mother had seemed like a heron, a bird we both loved, covered with oil slick and trapped forever. On the walk from the bus stop I met Michael, my closest friend. He asked me gently how my mother was doing. ''She's dying,'' I screamed at him. It was the first and only time during her illness that I heard those words.

Each of us has to face our own dying. My mother found her own way, and Eileen and you and I will have to find ours. Anna's way was uniquely involved with her relationship to Kirby. Through this highly intelligent and loyal animal, she came to awareness and acceptance of her dying. This is Anna and Kirby's story.

Kirby and Anna walked together every day while Anna was dying. There were six inches of snow at the beginning, twenty at the end, and with each step they sank into its coolness. The winter light bounced around on the white surfaces of branches and ground, enclosing them within circles. They moved as the light moved with them, parts of the pattern.

Kirby loved everything about this world—its cold, its light, its smell of clarity. He picked up the energy of winter and vibrated with it.

They walked the same path every afternoon, crossing a field, a stretch of woods, and a hill down to the lake. Although the lake was frozen, they never went past its rim. The rim was the point where the warmer land met the water, and the ice was thin and easily cracked by the animals who came to drink. This rim was their boundary.

When Anna walked through the woods with Kirby, she crossed a personal boundary. In the house, she was protected by warm air, nourishing food, and a familiar order. The row of medicine bottles on the kitchen shelf and the calendar filled with future doctors' appointments signified her continuous living. Everything in the house was designed to insure that she remain alive and that her life would be as it always had been. She would safely return to her old self, a self held in place by the structure of the household. Her role at this moment in the life of the household was to fight the cancer, because she couldn't continue to be there if she died.

Eileen's father, Peter, insisted that Anna fight, long after fighting had become irrelevant. It was not his fault. At the beginning the doctors assumed, as they are trained to do, that they could stop the cancer. They adopted the framework of war and proceeded to attack the cancer with all of their medical weapons. They spoke to Anna and Peter about how they had to attack it, conquer it, not give in. When one method failed, they moved on to another. When one doctor was uncertain, he called in others—tactical specialists, experts in the latest maneuvers. They were the generals, and Anna was their only soldier. It was she who fought through all the battles. Peter saw his role as sergeant, keeping her going.

The forms of combat in our society are excellent for teaching us how to win. They teach us to want to win against all odds, to not give up, to keep trying. Although athletics can also teach us how to lose, it is a form of loss that is intricately tied to the structure of winning. Loss in the context of winning means that you practice harder and struggle and do everything to prepare for the next battle. You never give up.

In the framework of war there is no place for feelings of peace and acceptance of loss. In real wars, and in medical battles, there is massive denial of the ultimate losses, the deaths. Death comes at the end of a brave struggle against it, and can then be experienced only as defeat. We cannot prepare for it because we are too busy fighting its arrival. We do not see it as inevitable, and therefore cannot accept it with inner peace.

At the beginning of the illness, Peter was Anna's sergeant and coach. He was there for her, fighting for her and suffering with her. And then, in the fifth month, the doctors found that the cancer had spread throughout her body. The cancer, the enemy, was now inseparable from Anna's body and Anna's self. It was time for acceptance.

But Peter could not shift his framework. He kept on fighting, and the battleground was Anna. He could not let her accept her self. With every look and touch meant to help her, he told her that any feeling of acceptance was defeat. In his presence, she felt guilty for not being stronger, for even thinking about leaving him and the children. Each look and touch kept her from feeling her way into dying. He begged her to live.

It was in this last month that Anna turned to Kirby. She needed Kirby to find within herself a way to accept her dying.

One morning when Eileen came down for breakfast, Anna was lying on the sofa unable to move. It was the first time she had not gotten up to be with the children. She felt as if a fog were inside her.

She had always liked the fog. But the fog she had known had been light and gentle, a cirrus cloud that would lower itself until it hovered like a spacecraft over a quiet field. The bits of water floated apart from each other, so that the whole cloud was open and permeable. When you reached out your hand, the mist touched it lightly, leaving the outline of your hand and the feeling of warmth within your skin intact. The old fog had touched her, leaving the core of herself alive and aware.

This new fog was very different. It was heavy and possessive, also like a spaceship, but now the alien presence felt dangerous to her. It reached inside her and then solidified, so that its presence took over all of her space, her inside warmth and center, and she couldn't feel herself. When she went to find herself, all she could feel was the doom of the fog.

Later that day, Kirby rose from his position next to the window and looked at her. It was nearing the time for their walk. He wasn't exactly restless, just expectant. His internal clock told him it was time. But he also knew that Anna's clock, or whatever it was that moved her into getting up, putting on layers of clothing, and opening the door, was not the same as his, and was almost always slower to arrive. There had been a few times when he wasn't ready and she'd roused him, excited and happy, wanting to go. But usually it was he who waited for her, and lately, he waited a long time. So he practiced patience, by watching her, watching for some sign from her eyes, her hands, her voice, that readiness was stirring inside her.

The fog didn't want her to go for a walk. It didn't want her to do anything. Kirby moved nearer and lay down next to her on the rug. She could see his shape at the edge of her left eye. Time passed. He shifted his head so that he could see her precisely. Although his body was calm and patient, his half-closed eyes were focused upon her. He was ready to go. She let his energy lift her, first just in her mind, then into actual motion, out of the fog. The fog was still with her, making her move awkwardly, in a rhythm that was both slow and erratic. But a tiny center, pierced by Kirby's look, had opened up and she was able to feel her self again.

In the woods, Kirby lay down in the snow the way light lies on water. Small shadows of brush and twigs fell on his thick coat and on the white ground. In the afternoon light there were almost no colors. It was like night vision, different shades of black and white, and when the sun hit the ice, it was like star-light. There was the white ice, the white snow, the light gray bushes and the dark gray trees, the lighter and darker shadows on the white snow, and the gray and white dog. And there was her. She was there, still existing.

It would be so much easier, so much less painful here, Anna thought. She had a vision of Kirby when it was time for him to die. He lay down in the snow, digging a place which wrapped his body perfectly in white cold, and he circled the place, around and around, until it was patted down and leveled just right, and then he flopped down in the center, resting his large heavy head on the comforting ground, and he died. She told Eileen about this vision, and then she told her the story of Queequeg, who built his own coffin because he knew he would die at sea. But Kirby was on the ground, in a world where he belonged, and his burial place would be a shape in the earth that curved perfectly with the shape of his body in its last position. She wondered if he would curl up, with his head on a paw, or stretch out, with his neck vulnerable. But he would be alone at the time of death, and vulnerability would be irrelevant. There would be no enemies, no others. The snow, the woods, the lake, the branches would spread out in all directions in endless white. There would be no motion. Kirby would lie down, and he would be part of the stillness, part of the whole. He would feel the unity of everything.

She felt how simple it would be to lie down and become a tree trunk, a shadow, a part of the whole. She swayed slightly and grabbed her stick. The sudden motion of her hand, and the energy needed to keep herself balanced, brought her back to a sense of separation. She was Anna, wife of Peter, mother of Alex, age thirteen, and Eileen, age ten. They needed her to walk back to the house and resume her role in the family structure. She pictured Eileen running across the field with Kirby, both of them strong and free. How would Eileen grow up without her? What price would her children pay for her death?

She looked at Kirby. He was watching her, waiting to see if she was ready to leave. They stared at each other for a moment. He got up and came over to her side. She leaned some of her weight into him.

Donald Winnicott said that a good therapist provides a holding environment for a patient. The space between therapist and patient is completely safe; whatever happens, she will not fall. If her soul is fragmented, the therapist will hold the pieces in the connection between them until she can integrate them. She will not fall apart.

Perhaps this is why Christ as a baby appears weightless to Medieval painters and sculptors. Mary holds him, as all mothers hold their infants, in trust and safety. But other mothers have to worry about falls. The space between Mary and Jesus, the holding environment, is held by God. They are both able to float.

Later, on the cross and after death in Mary's arms, Christ takes on weight. He suffers and cries out to his father, "Why hast thou forsaken me?" In Michelangelo's *Pieta*, Mary bends over, head bent, back bent, her whole body bending to balance his enormous weight.

Anna, in her illness, was filled with weights. The cancer drained her of energy. The fog penetrated her. The fear of death was itself a weight. When guilt was added, Anna could barely move from heaviness.

At the beginning she had to be strong to fight the cancer. In the middle she had to be hopeful, speaking of the future and responding to plans for

next month or next year as if she would be there. Toward the end, when talking was difficult and hope was hard even for Peter to pretend, her responsibility was to not die. They asked her, in words and silently, to keep herself alive. She needed to be able to go, and they did not know how to let her.

Being with Kirby lifted the weight. When he died he would return to the natural world which he loved and belonged to. When she died, he would let her go.

Kirby gave her a holding environment. It was not exactly that Kirby held her, but that the two of them were held by the natural world. With Kirby she was connected without having to hold herself together. The universe held her.

It snowed all day and night, and the new layer of soft snow made Anna want to walk even more than usual. She walked slowly, stopping often to touch the snow. Kirby ran ahead and back, flopping like a puppy.

At the edge of the woods, a set of tracks crossed their path, and they followed it. Two patterns, larger paws and smaller, were clear in the fresh snow. And then there was a circle of fusion, the sharp separation between the larger and smaller pattern of tracks suddenly merging, so that orderly spaces between front and back paws and large and small paws collapsed, leaving marks touching, overlapping, and

absorbing each other. The lucid pattern ended in a spiral of confusion.

Kirby sniffed deeply. He buried his nose in the circle to examine the event. His interest was so intense that Anna ignored her need to rest and went over to join him. Kirby had moved beyond the visual pattern of the paws and into some deeper level that his sniffing was revealing. When Anna got close, she could see three tufts of fur, each about an inch long and less than a quarter of an inch in width, of a brown and gray mixture. Kirby, however, was focused on a patch of snow that looked the same as the other patches in the circle. Anna knelt next to him. There, in the patch, were two tiny dots of red blood. Kirby had found the circle's pattern, the end of the spiral. They stared down together at the moment of merging, when the smaller animal had disappeared into the larger. There it was: the moment of death.

It didn't seem so awful, so emotionally draining, as it did in human contexts. It seemed very calm. Cold and quiet, like the snow. The small animal had entered the whole in a different form. The hovering emotions didn't make sense here. There was, during the struggle, fear and desperation and probably, just before the end, a freezing of all feeling, a total numbing. And then there was the calm; it was over, and with the end of breath came the end of emotion.

But we know there is sadness in the animal world. I remember watching an elephant linger over the body of a dead antelope, aware of the warm body that could no longer breathe, aware of the end of the body's motion. And I saw a dove standing by the side of the road after its mate was hit by a car; the bird stood there, in spite of the onrushing cars which ordinarily would have caused it to flee, and waited. It was waiting for the body to respond in some familiar way, to breathe, to coo, to lift its wings and fly back to safety. It waited for any sign of life. It must have been feeling something as it waited, a feeling of expectancy that we would call hope; and it must have begun to feel a sense of confusion, maybe a sense of defeat, when there was no response. At the moment just before it flew off, when something inside told it that the waiting was over, it must have felt a sense of ending. It was the end of a connection, in which the two of them had flown together, found food together, made babies together. In that moment when the end was sensed, it must have felt something like despair.

These are the two poles of dying, the peaceful connection to the whole and the despairing separation. They are not specifically animal or human poles; they are part of the dying of all living creatures. With Peter and her children, Anna felt mostly the despairing pole. Being with Kirby in the animal world brought her to the other side. She needed that side to live out her dying.

I found myself feeling the despairing pole all over again as I listened to Eileen. Not all the time, of course, but at moments. One day I had an intense longing to bring my mother back, just for her last six months; but this time I would get her a German shepherd. In my daydream my mother and this large, incredibly protective dog go everywhere together. He sits on her bed in the hospital, guarding her from fear.

One day near the end of her illness, Anna and Kirby had gone through the woods and were stepping carefully down the slope to the lake when Anna saw it. It was a flash, up by the edge of the woods, in the corner of her eye. It was impossible to recognize it; it came very fast and low to the ground, so low that it probably wasn't a bird, but it might have been. Kirby focused. The woods were silent. The flash of motion had disappeared.

They continued down the hill to the edge of the lake. And then there was a thrashing of bushes and a pounding of ground coming through the woods down to the water. They couldn't see anything; there was only the noise. After a minute, a gray shape leapt from the woods onto the lake and ran for the opposite shore. Then a second shape, also gray and the same size as the first, leapt onto the lake and into sight. They ran fast and freely once clear of the crowded woods. But there was still noise coming from the woods, and then they saw why: a third gray shape was coming out of the woods above the point where the other two had left it, running hard over the lake to catch them. Three gray wolves had come to Anna and Kirby from out of the wilderness. They must have been very hungry in this cold winter and decided to cross the lake. Kirby watched them quietly. He did not make any move to chase or join them. They were about his height, but thinner and faster. He watched them for a long time, as did Anna, until they were totally out of sight. And then for a while he and Anna were silent and motionless, as if they both felt that something important had happened.

The wolves were a turning point for Anna. Very few living humans had ever seen wolves in this part of the country. Anna knew she would never see them again. They were wild and free, and very hungry. They lived with the immediate possibility of death—from hunger, from a broken leg, from an infected wound, from a gun. Although she and Kirby would not have hurt them, they had run for their lives, and would always have to do this. Death was with them always, in the daily, ordinary moments of their lives.

And they were free. Death did not break them. They moved like the wind to avoid it, but they moved in freedom. In the form of a gray shape moving across her field of vision, she took inside her the edge of freedom. It was an edge, a sliver like the new moon, but it was there now. It was freedom within the nearness of death.

Kirby was also profoundly affected. There had been a moment when Anna had thought he would try to chase them, even catch them. And then, would he want to join them? Would he want to run into the wilderness and leave the craziness of his human life, tied inextricably to a dying woman, watching her, guarding her, waiting. For a moment she thought he would leave her, or want to leave her. Even while focused intensely on the wolves, she had watched him too.

But he had not wanted to leave; it had never been even a momentary impulse. He had a purpose as singular and focused as that of the wolves. The wolves and Kirby were very close to each other, very similar.

The wolves had affected Kirby, but not in the way that Anna had at first imagined. He had felt their energy, and the woods that he had come to accept as safe and familiar had taken on a wild and dangerous feeling. Now he reacted intensely to every motion—the blowing of a twig, the landing of a bird—motions which he would normally have let flow through his calm awareness. Like the wolves, he was looking for danger.

They turned at the same time to go back. It was as if they were both overcome by the energy of the encounter and needed to return to home base to absorb it. The walk back was especially difficult this day for Anna. The snow was deep and her strength was waning. She stopped frequently to lean against trees.

That night Anna spoke to her children about her dying. Alex, trying to follow his father's model, at first would not listen. He said that if Anna did not think she was going to die, it would not happen. But Anna, for the first time, was free of guilt and confusion. There was a clarity in her voice that compelled her son to listen. And as soon as he opened his attention, he understood.

Eileen had always been listening. She sat with her head pressed against her mother's chest, hearing her voice through the echoing of their bodies. Eileen, who had been open to her mother's fear and confusion from the beginning of the illness, knew the truth.

Anna told her children that she was going to die. And then she told them the story of meeting the wolves. The children listened intently. When she had finished, they all felt a sense of oneness, as if they were the wolf pack, running across the frozen lake, together and free.

In the middle of the night, Anna got up to get some water. She found Eileen on the floor, curled against Kirby, sleeping. Kirby lifted his large heavy head to look up at her. "Stay," Eileen heard her whisper.

Once Anna was free, she talked to the children a lot, whenever she had the strength, about her walks with Kirby, about her childhood, about her dying. Alex listened intensely, as if each sound was a precious stone that he needed to hold on to. Eileen heard these words also, and someplace in her mind she stored them, or fragments of them, together with the images, the shapes and smells. But most important, she stored the feelings, Anna's awe and wonder as she uncovered each new awareness. And when Eileen later put together Anna's story, she remembered clearly and certainly her mother's sense of peace at the end.

Anna died a week after seeing the wolves. Kirby lived for eight more years, a long time for a shepherd. He and Eileen often took that same walk together, across the field, through the woods, and down to the rim of the lake. Kirby died the winter that Eileen went away to college. No one said this at the time, but it seems clear that he knew he could leave then. Eileen understood this. She holds Kirby and her mother now, in her memory.

We are all afraid of our dying. We are entering, alone, a kind of space and time we have never experienced. We don't know what will happen to us, to our body and our self. We may have had near-death experiences, or dreams or visions of peacefulness and oneness after death. But even for those of us who are unafraid most of the time, there are moments of terror, when the unknown rips through us. Judith Herman, a psychologist who has studied men and women in situations of trauma, says that in moments of extreme terror soldiers call out to God or to their mothers. They call out to the two beings who can keep them from disintegration, their holding environment.

Animals are also afraid of dying. They experience the same moments of terror. But the fear comes for them just before the actual death, or near-death; they don't anticipate, for months or years before the actual time, their dying. Humans expect, anticipate, but we don't know. When we really know, we are able to accept our death as any animal does. It is the combination of anticipating and not-knowing that tortures us. A very sick animal will crawl into a crevice of the earth and either heal or die. We rush from one doctor to another, one emotional state to another: fight, give in; hope, despair; live, die.

If animals died in a different way from humans, we wouldn't feel the kind of intense connection to them that we do. If they died like machines, for instance—one morning you go out to your car and it has just stopped turning over—you would feel a different kind of connection. When an old car dies, we can feel the sadness of losing a daily companion. But we don't pick up the car's suffering and resonate with it. Or, if we do, it is because we identify the car's body with an animal's body or our own body, a vulnerable, permeable organism that feels its destruction as pain. When that destruction reaches a certain point, the body can no longer hold itself together as a moving, breathing entity. And when the body loses its integrated structure, we don't know what happens to us, our center, our soul.

Animals die exactly as we do. We have the same kind of body, and the same experience of terror and pain. An animal's understanding of time and death may be different from ours, and different from one species to another, but the feelings are the same. This is the essence of the human-animal connection, the same sense of aliveness at the core. And this is the essence of animal-human death, the same terror of the destruction of the body and the end of aliveness.

Animals handle this ending better than we do. They sink into the earth and let it hold them. In the passage of dying, their holding environment is the earth, which is always there for them. This is how Kirby helped Anna to die. He gave her that holding environment. He helped her to feel her connection to the universe, and an inner peace, at the end.

10

FREEDOM

SHE was a baby when I met her, sitting in a cage in the corner of the shaman's stall in the Guadalajara market. She sat to the right of the shaman, watching him with her left eye. When I approached the stall from her left she focused on me intently, but when I approached quietly from her right, she didn't turn. She saw emptiness with her right eye.

Early in her life, hunters had gone into the mountains with bows and arrows. With a single arrow, one of them took out her eye. When she fell to the ground, and he saw what he had done, he gasped. It is not good to kill an eagle. He took off his shirt and felt fear in his chest. The baby eagle lay on the ground in pain and terror. She flapped her wings, trying to fly away; but she was too young, just a baby. Smoothing her wings against her sides, the man wrapped her in his shirt and brought her to the shaman.

"It was an accident," he whispered, over and over, like the Ancient Mariner. The shaman listened. The man knew that he had been careless. He had shot high into a tree without knowing where his arrow would go. He had acted without intent, without awareness. But he did not have any bad intention. He had not meant to harm the spirits of the forest. So the shaman released his guilt by taking the baby eagle from him, taking his burden.

The shaman could not bring back Neti-Neti's eye. But he could help her to grow, to become strong, and perhaps one day to fly back to her world.

Each day I went to the shaman's stall to be with him. I watched him with the people who came for help. The stall was lined with plants that could heal. There were two rows of small jars filled with powdered herbs. Behind these jars were larger containers with leaves of autumn colors—brown, deep red, dark green. Way in the back were enormous jars filled with whole roots and barks.

On the counter were three gray stone mortar bowls with pestles, a mixing bowl, and a balance scale. Beside the scale was a set of weights, cylinders of lead carefully ordered in a wooden case. The stall smelled like the hay in a freshly mowed field.

Sick, frightened people came to the shaman. The stall was on a central path of the crowded market, with hundreds of people walking by each day. But if one of these people was coming to see him, he knew. He looked toward them as they came into sight, and watched them walking toward him. He knew a great deal about them before they reached the stall, before they spoke.

He invited them to sit on one of the stools and he listened to their stories with complete attention. Sometimes he touched them, on their heads, their stomachs, wherever they felt the trouble. He looked into their eyes. Then he took down jars and ground the plants in the stone bowls. He placed each powder in the right bucket of the scale, put a weight in the left bucket, and added more powder until the scale balanced. He poured each powder into his mixing bowl and stirred them together.

He transferred the mixture into a brown paper bag and handed it to each person. Then he explained how to take the powder. Each of his movements was filled with care. His voice, coming from the depths of his fluid body, rolled through their bodies. He sent soothing, rhythmic waves, holding them in his space. They began to relax. They entered his rhythm. They took his vibrancy, as much as they were able, and it lifted their fear as sun lifts fog. Safe in the space of his rhythm, they let go of their fear and felt their own centers, their own energy. They left with the bag pressed to their bodies, his spirit glowing in their hearts.

I went to see this transformation. I too was transformed by being there with him.

The shaman taught me how to feed Neti-Neti the only thing she would eat, very fresh raw meat. Sometimes he would ask me to watch the stall for a while, and she and I would be alone. I talked to her.

One day he asked me if I would take her home. He said that she would be better staying with me, out of a cage and away from the noisy market. He said: "You will heal her."

Soren and I were staying in an old Spanish house with our friend, Douglas, who was at that time a medical student at the University of Guadalajara. We were one of four families sharing the house, two downstairs and two above. The rooms on the lower level opened onto a central courtyard with a garden and a tiny pond. We were on the upper level, with a balcony that went around the garden on all four sides. We shared the upper level with an old woman who had a family of songbirds. The birds lived in large and small cages on her side of the balcony. On the other side, we set up a perch for Neti-Neti.

The shaman was right, of course. Neti-Neti was more relaxed here. She was free of the cage, outdoors, feeling the wind, learning about the sky over her head. She was part of the world to which she belonged, the moon and the sun rising and setting, the stars with her at night. From her perch she could see the mountains in the distance. She came alive here. We fixed a chain from her leg to the perch to keep her from leaving before it was safe for her to go.

The shaman gave me a pair of gloves for protection. They were thick black leather, falcon gloves, and had been scratched and softened by years of contact with powerful claws. When I wore an old woolen jacket and the gloves, I could hold her.

She had no intention of hurting me—she was a baby, and I was the one who fed her. But if she had grabbed my bare hand in her talons, she would have broken the skin. It was the same reflexive hold as that of a baby monkey and baby human clinging to hair. She grasped to keep herself balanced, to keep from falling.

At first, when I approached her, she would move away from my body, going as far as the perch would let her. I talked to her quietly, many times each day. And each day, at sunset, I fed her, holding the raw meat in my gloved hand above her beak as she stretched her neck to grasp it.

One day I approached her and she didn't move away. I put my gloved hand next to her chest and she raised one claw, gripped my hand, and then brought the other claw forward to perch on me. She stood looking at me with her left eye, balanced and alert.

I talked to her for a while. I told her about the mountains and the high cliffs which were her home. I told her about the cold air, the strong winds, the snow. I gave her a vision of the place where she might be one day.

She stirred and started to move up my arm. Absorbed in the vision and the excitement of holding her, I was not attending to my arm. I was not wearing the jacket. She moved one claw from the glove to the bare skin of my arm and clasped tightly. I let out a scream. Poor baby eagle—she had no idea why I was screaming, but she knew something was wrong. My arm was shaking and she dug deeper into my flesh to steady herself, looking at me, turning her head to see the space around us with her one eye, trying to figure out what was wrong.

Once the initial shock was over I was able to handle the pain, and I very carefully moved my arm next to the perch and begged her to step onto it. When she withdrew her talons the pain surged up again, but I was prepared this time and didn't scream.

I have been bitten by animals, but there is only one other time that I have been gripped as intensely as I was by Neti-Neti. It happened with Panda about five years later.

Soren, Panda, and I were living in New Jersey when Soren, who was then eleven years old, got a trail bike. We used to put the bike in the backseat of a huge old Pontiac and drive to the wetlands, where there were waving cattails and miles of trails weaving among them.

The bike, a sturdy old Honda, was very noisy, and Panda hated noise. Like all of us, he was startled by loud sudden noises, but unlike many of us, he did not adapt to the sound. He stayed frightened and upset until we could get away.

On the first several trips to the wetlands, Soren

went off on the bike and Panda and I stayed behind, waiting. I wanted to walk through the fields with Panda, but he was too nervous; he just wanted to stand exactly where he was until Soren returned. He didn't run after Soren only because he didn't want to leave me alone.

On our third trip, after a few runs, Soren asked me if I wanted a ride on the bike. When I make a mistake with an animal it is usually because I am focusing on something else. Soren's invitation had surprised me. I was thinking, Does he know how much harder it is to balance the bike with another person on the back? Is he skilled enough to do it? Should we take the chance? I was looking at the bike, looking at Soren, who was thin but strong. I said "Sure" and swung my leg over the back of the seat.

Panda ran over next to my left leg. Soren started the engine, which roared as usual, and Panda began to bark, not a mildly upset bark, but a frantic, serious-danger bark. But I didn't really tune into his feeling. I was focusing on Soren, on the bike, on my own balance; I was already feeling the happiness of rushing through fields on a motorcycle. Soren started rolling forward and Panda lunged. He grabbed my thigh in his jaws to save me. I screamed; Soren cut the engine and Panda let go of my leg.

The motorcycle was a lion, I was a lamb, and Panda was saving my life. He gripped me with all his power. His teeth broke the skin and went deep enough for him to hold tight; it took several months

for the wound to heal. Because of Neti-Neti, I recognized this grip. It is a deeply powerful, deeply connecting grip.

So I learned not to forget the jacket with Neti-Neti.
Under its protective layer, holding her felt wonderful. I was holding her and she was holding me. The
strength of her hold, the power of her grip, became
part of our connection.

She always started on my hand, but my wrist
wasn't strong and after a few minutes my hand wob-
bled. She would then move up to my arm, feeling
its shape as her ground. She moved around on my
arm until she found a place that was steady and then
she stayed there. She never tried, as parrots do, to
climb onto my shoulder or head.

I gave her my right arm so that she could see
me clearly with her left eye. This was what she
wanted. While grounded on me, she always
watched me.

It was the same with me. It was not fear, not
distrust, between us. It was an understanding of the
power of the other, the difference of the other.
Without awareness, we could accidentally, uninten-
tionally, hurt each other. We could lose an eye.

She accepted my voice, my presence, my body
as a ground. But she did not want me to touch her.
When I stroked the feathers on her chest lightly, she
turned her head and tried to ignore me.

I touched her for my own sake, not hers. I was intent on healing her. Today, I would not touch her. I didn't know back then how to give her energy without actual physical contact. I instinctively knew that touch was very important for me—my way of transferring energy to her, of building energy between us, of bringing us strength. So I stroked her. And after a few weeks she came to accept it as part of our connection. I think she just got used to it, the way I got used to Hogahn's swamp smell. But I grew to love Hogahn's smell. Neti-Neti accepted my touch, but I doubt that she ever loved it.

Neti-Neti could not be hugged around the neck like a horse or slept with like a dog. Holding each other was difficult and even dangerous. But that was part of our relationship, touching the difference between us.

Soren used to play every day with the children of a family who kept ducks, and one day the children's father gave him two baby ducks to raise. At first I was nervous about the ducks being around Neti-Neti. I put their corn and water behind the bathroom door, safely away from her. But they were not afraid of her. They wandered freely throughout the compound, on the balcony and into the rooms, pecking at the tiles and the cracks between them for anything edible. But they always returned to Neti-Neti, to the space near her perch and within her sight. They slept below her perch at night.

One day, one of the ducks fell off the balcony down to the courtyard below. It must have landed on a sharp rock, and it died. Soren and I were not home at the time, but Douglas tried to save it. Then, because he was a medical student, he decided to dissect the duck and feed it to Neti-Neti.

She wouldn't eat it. She turned her head away. It was fresh raw meat and she wouldn't touch it. She knew it was the baby duck.

I have been told that some people who raise animals such as pigs for food can have a personal relationship with the animals while they are growing up, then turn off their feelings in order to kill them or send them to their death at a slaughterhouse. It is sometimes said that this approach is the way of the natural world, in which creatures kill and eat other creatures. But Neti-Neti made me question this view. Perhaps it is only the human mind that is capable of this kind of separation: first we are part of the same family, connected in danger and wellbeing; then we are different, one of us superior, one of us taking the other's life. Neti-Neti, a predatory bird, a born hunter and eater of flesh, did not make that separation; the duck remained part of her family even after death, and she did not eat it.

Birds in the wild have to fly. It is their only means of escape from danger. But they also have to descend to the ground, where they are surrounded by danger, because they need to eat. Their food lies in the earth, but their home is above, in high trees and the sky.

Land creatures are usually dangerous to birds, but birds are safe with some mammals. In China egrets stay close to water buffalo in the rice fields, feeding on bugs from the buffalo's coat. On Kauai the white egrets stay with the horses. They are safe with these large, powerful animals. If any other creature approaches, they fly away.

The aerodynamics of a bird's wing is perfect. But in this perfection, if even the smallest thing goes wrong, it is almost irreparable. Once a bird's wing is injured, it rarely flies again.

This has caused me fear and anger throughout my life when I have tried to help injured birds. Any other kind of injury will heal, but not the one most needed, the only one essential for survival. The wing is like the spinal cord. We cannot fix it.

I have accepted wounds and suffering as part of the life cycle. Still, when I see a bird that is very alive but cannot fly, it upsets me. I sometimes try to put the bird up in a tree to get it away from predators. But then it will not be able to eat.

When you think of the stuffed animals we give to children, they are rarely birds. We give all different kinds of animals—bears, rabbits, seals, elephants; we even give lizards and colorful worms. When we give a stuffed bird, it is one that we usually see walking on the ground, a duck or a penguin. I don't think I have ever seen a stuffed animal meant for a child that was a bird with its wings spread. We don't give children eagles or sparrows in flight.

I think that we have a feeling, deep in our core, about the fragility of wings. Stuffed animals are meant to be hugged, dragged along the ground, dropped and picked up. Their bodies are generally soft and round. The legs of teddy bears get broken and fall off, and we accept this. We make a splint or sew the limb back. But we cannot accept the breaking of wings in flight. We don't give children stuffed birds with outstretched wings because we know that the wings will eventually break, and we cannot fix a broken wing.

And there is something inside us that does not want to pretend. We don't want to put a splint on the wing, pretending we can fix it. There is something inside us that connects the fragile, delicate wing to pure freedom. We tell our children stories, and we sing them songs, of birds in flight. In our stories birds fly away, from pain, from suffering, from being trapped. They fly freely to other worlds, other realities. We don't want to take this knowledge away from our children. We don't want to give them broken wings.

Neti-Neti was a rare success story. This was partly due to the shaman's wisdom and partly because her wings had never been injured. She lost her eye, but she could survive with that loss. The healing that occurred between Neti-Neti, the shaman, and me was not a miracle. It was the healing of the shock, the fear, the disorientation Neti-Neti had experienced in losing her family and her mountain home. It was a physical, psychological, and spiritual healing; all healings are. She found the inner balance to use her wings, finding her self.

When the shaman thought she was almost ready, we put Neti-Neti in a large room, took off her leg chain, and left her alone. We watched her from the balcony window. She spread her wings.

Soren and I gasped. We had not known the enormity of her wingspan. She had never spread her wings while the chain was around her. She filled the room with magnificent feathers. Energy radiated from her outstretched tips.

The shaman smiled. "You did well," he said.

"Can we set her free?" Soren asked.

"Not yet," he said. "But soon, at full moon. I want her to practice using her one eye with her wings spread, to swivel."

Every day we brought her into the room and left her alone there. She learned to turn while her wings were spread in order to see the other side of the world.

Neti-Neti knew that her stay with us was temporary. You may think that I am projecting. Since knowing Neti-Neti, I have seen, touched, and talked to many wild animals in captivity. Most of them know, at their core, their state of freedom. They know that they are wounded and that the person helping them intends to let them free when they are able to move again. Or they know that the person is caging them, for some reason they often do not understand, and they try their best to escape. Of course, like us, they are sometimes mistaken about the person's intentions. But I have found that their understanding is usually accurate.

When a wounded animal knows that you intend to set it free, it does not struggle to escape. It stays quiet, giving all of its energy to the healing process. The two of you are healing together, the only way healing can take place.

If the animal senses that you have taken away its freedom, it may not heal at all. It may choose to die. Healing only happens when the wounded being wants to be healed.

Healing is a connection of energy between a creature and the universe. The healer is an intermediary, someone who helps. The healer's presence—her body and the spirit at the core of herself—helps to bring the creature back into harmony with the universe. If the animal senses that the person who is helping is also a person to be feared, a person who will take away its freedom, the animal may choose a different way of harmony: the peace of death.

Neti-Neti sensed that the chain on her leg was temporary, a way of keeping her safely in the nest. She already understood the sky. She watched the sun rising from behind the close mountains, her home. She knew that the stone transformed from gray to blue and purple and back to gray again as the sun traveled over her head and descended behind the far mountain peaks. In the darkness she watched the moon, which grew rounder and rounder, then disappeared, then swelled again. She was in touch with her freedom.

I think that freedom is a necessity for shamans; that is why they are so close to animals. Neti-Neti tuned into the shaman and picked up the freedom at his core. She knew that they shared the awareness of freedom. She never struggled, with him or with me. She did not need to escape. She knew that when she was ready she would be in the sky.

One day Serge King, who teaches the shamanic tradition of Huna, was talking about the love of freedom in shamans and animals, and a woman named Claudette told us this story. Her dog was in quarantine on Hawaii for the required four months and she went every day to sit with him so he would know that he hadn't been abandoned. For four months she sat in the kennels, listening to the sounds of the dogs. She said that there were four barks that she was able to distinguish. There was a bark when food was arriving, a bark when a visitor was approaching, and a bark when it was time to be walked on a leash in the yard. But when a dog escaped, when a dog somehow got outside of the prison and was running free, there was a different bark. She said it was a bark of joyousness. It was pure joy for the dog who had gotten free, and a powerful resonating to his freedom. She said the sound of that barking was different from every other sound.

Under an almost full moon I went to talk to Neti-Neti. As I talked she stared up at the moon. I told her that the next evening she would be going home.

I stroked Neti-Neti for the last time, feeling her heartbeat beneath my gloved fingers and watching her amazing feathers in the light of the moon. She tolerated my touch as usual. I stayed a long time and she didn't move away.

The next morning the shaman, Douglas, Soren, and I drove to the mountains. We drove for three hours, first on a paved road and then on a dirt one. The smooth hard dirt became a rutted passageway through a landscape of rocks and cactus. We left the car and walked into the mountains. Neti-Neti rode on the shaman's left shoulder, tied at her leg to his belt.

I watched her excitement, how she kept turning her head, flexing her claws. She knew it was
time. The thing that surprised me was that she didn't
try to fly away when we got out of the car or when
we were climbing into the foothills. She trusted that
in the right moment, we would let her be free.

We reached the top of a high hill overlooking a
valley and the higher cliffs of the mountains. We
were at the highest point on the hill. Neti-Neti suddenly became very calm. From the shaman's shoulder, she looked at me. She looked directly at me for
a long time. We said good-bye.

The shaman unlatched the chain and she
moved from his shoulder to his gloved hand. He
stretched out his hand toward the mountains. She
spread her wings, and she was flapping them, flapping them rigorously, but not moving from his
hand. I held my breath. Then she entered the air,
rising over our heads and above the hill, over the
valley, into the cool, clear mountain air, soaring toward the high cliffs. I let out my breath, and in the
stillness, I could hear the shaman chanting to her,
blessing her flight. We watched her long after she
was out of sight, over the ridge of the eagle cliffs.

I watch her still, her wings, her claws, her seeing eye. She grips my soul.

11

HARMONY

ONE night on Kauai I went down to Salt Pond to see Raymond. Stray creatures, animals who once belonged somewhere, make their way to Raymond's van. They seem to know that they can trust him. I've seen dogs who would not come within forty feet of another human come and eat from Raymond's bowl.

Sometimes dogs who really need a pack stay with Raymond. These dogs are hungry and frightened. When they arrive they are so full of pain that no one wants to be around them. Raymond keeps them for a while. They eat, they play with Raymond's dog, Buddy, and they begin to feel safe and happy. People see them relating to Raymond as loyal and intelligent companions. They adopt them.

Lady was a small, thin, older dog who was starving when she found Raymond's van. She lived safely with him for several months and then she died.

When I got to the van the Sunday of her death it was dusk, two people were leaving, and Raymond was asleep. The people pointed to a blanket and told me that Lady's body was wrapped inside.

I wasn't sure what to do. I never stay alone at the beach at night. But I wasn't alone; Raymond was in the van and Buddy was next to me. Still, I was nervous. I began walking around the campsite, collecting bottles and straightening up a little. Buddy watched me nervously. When I took some plates down to the water he went with me and sat beside me at the water's edge. I thought of Penelope and Joannie. Whatever feelings he had about Lady's death had probably been intensified by Raymond's grief and my nervousness. He stayed by my side.

Buddy is the coolest of dogs. He never pushes himself on you. But tonight he was upset and needed me. I decided to stay for a while. I lay down under the stars and Buddy lay next to me.

So many stars were visible that night. The tension of the day which had ended in Lady's death gradually dissolved under the silent sky. I felt Buddy slowly calm as we looked at the night.

We were next to the reef, and the only sounds were the waves breaking on coral and our own breathing. The lights from town and the buoys that guide boats into the harbor were far behind us.

On the beach at night it is easy to be anywhere. The separations between earth and sky, land and water dissolve in the darkness. No ordinary-world landmarks anchor you down. I went through one of the stars and into another world of glowing vibrations. I left my body safe and warm in Buddy's care.

When I came back, I was quiet and only lightly attached to the world of Salt Pond. But Buddy had stayed on the beach, in the sand, with Lady's body as well as mine. I got up to leave, assuming that Buddy would let me go quietly. Instead he did something really strange: he started to play with me. Like a puppy, he leapt up my leg and tried to knock me down.

At first I didn't understand and I kept walking. Buddy had never played with me like this. Dogs select people for clear, strong qualities, just as humans do, and Buddy had not selected me for playfulness.

He was quite accurate in this assessment: I was not playful. I wanted to be, but I was part of a human world where I didn't feel I belonged. I was nervous about other people's reactions, afraid I would say or do the wrong thing. I wasn't secure enough to be playful.

But that night Buddy wanted to play with me. And he trusted me enough to play-attack. So I play-attacked back, letting him drop me to the sand and leap on me. We rolled over and under the stars, wrestling away sadness.

Years of training in the separation of mind and body would have let me resolve my sadness by calming my mind. Buddy wanted to feel calm through body and mind together. He wanted to feel connected to me by moving in harmony with me. He wanted our bodies to resonate together.

Buddy and I played that night, and in our play, we restored the joy of being alive, the happiness of being related. Lady's spirit was at one with the universe.

In his study of infants and mothers, Daniel Stern speaks of the motions of mother and child as a dance. The infant tunes into the mother's emotional rhythms and moves in harmony with her. The infant not only senses her feelings, but moves its body to the rhythms of these feelings.

The motion of the body to the rhythms of feelings is the first dance. In the first dance, we bring our whole self—body and mind—into harmony with the other. In the earliest dance, and throughout our lives, we move in connection with others— a mother, a lover, a tribe.

The play of animals develops from this first, infant-mother dance. Muky jumps on Sasha and she jumps back, matching his rhythm and its intensity. They play-bite and play-growl while leaping on top of each other. The movements are choreographed as a real fight, but without the harm. When Sasha pins Muky on the ground, she lets him up gently and the dance is over.

Muky and Sasha are always playing. They race over the field in back of the house on City Island, running in freedom and feeling the incredible energy of flying over the ground. Then if Sasha is in front, she finds a hiding place and crouches behind it. Muky runs up and is ambushed.

This is life for Muky and Sasha. This is not a special time they take out of their normal, serious working day. This is not running to get in shape or running to relax. This is just running. They love to run. They are totally inside the action of running. They *are* the running.

If you watch animals long enough, you see that play, dance, and work are essentially the same for them. These words are just different human names for the things that animals do. And this is important, because when we are really in tune with ourselves and the universe, they are the same for us too.

Imagine making love with someone you love and who loves you. It is play and it is absolutely serious. It is partly ritual and partly spontaneous, dancing together.

This is how Buddy buries a bone at Salt Pond. Another dog coming along cannot distract him. He is focused on getting the bone to the right spot. He works swiftly and effectively at digging the hole. He is very serious, but he's having a wonderful time. You can feel the joyful energy as his paws fling the dirt to the boundaries of the space that becomes the hole. He is doing the bone-burying dance.

If you've ever done exactly the right thing in an

emergency, you know how it feels to be totally inside the motion. You just move: you pull the child out of the water; you steer the speeding car into and through the skid. In the moment of action you are not feeling fear or anxiety or anything else. The feeling at the core of the self *is* the motion.

Animals move this way much of the time. They don't have our intervening hesitancies, the conflicts within ourselves that hold us back.

In most human cultures, we live split within ourselves, split between mind and body. We are taught early that the mind is separate from the body, and not only separate, but superior. The inferior body is blamed for desiring all the bodily pleasures, sensuous and sexual, that the culture is struggling to suppress. The superior mind is given the work of keeping the inferior, sometimes even sinful, body under control.

To make each of us conform, the culture uses our deepest fear: rejection. We are terrified of being shut out by our group. In the newborn creature, animal and human, rejection means death. If the mother pushes the infant away it cannot nurse and starves to death. If the pack abandons a young one, it cannot survive on its own.

Intertwined and inseparable from this physical need for connection is the emotional need to belong. Belonging means tuning in to another living creature who responds to you. Belonging is dancing and playing together.

Even in the relative physical safety of ordinary

life we carry our basic fear of rejection. We are afraid of being shut out of the group. And in human society, there are endless ways in which people can reject us. A look, a silence, can mean disapproval. In some relationships, that disapproval is enough to make us feel isolated and unsafe. In human society, fear of rejection is used to cut us off from the core of ourselves. We are trained not to do things because they might be "embarrassing." We are trained not to be in touch with ourselves, not to dance, not to do what we want with our lives, because others would not approve.

Animals do not lose touch with the core of themselves. They do not reject each other for being themselves. They express through the body, through the motions of the body, whatever they are feeling. They don't disconnect from each other or from themselves.

Animals keep their mind and body connected. Some people think that animals are only their bodies, or are so predominantly their bodies that they are incapable of disconnecting. But if you have ever been with an animal who is seriously wounded you know that it can disconnect. You can feel the terror when it realizes that its body is unable to move, unable to escape. It is not that animals are too simple to disconnect. It is that disconnection is a terrible thing for them, and happens only in the most extreme situations.

Once while Hogahn was living with me, he was trying to cross a busy road and ran head-on into the side of a moving car. A friend of mine at a car dealership saw the accident from the showroom window and rushed to help him. My friend and the vet were both surprised that he'd lived.

When I picked Hogahn up he was only partly conscious. Because he had a concussion, the vet did not give him any medication. At home on the couch, his head would slowly lower, wanting to rest, but he would jerk it up when it reached a certain angle. He must have felt extreme pain when he tried to lower it. I propped up pillows, but he couldn't use them. He held his head up the whole night.

The next day he closed himself off from everything, keeping all of his focus within, using all of his strength to heal. I sat with him, and toward evening watched him beginning to respond to a few things around him. He focused his eyes on my eyes. He moved his ears to the sound of my voice. He lapped up water. He was responding very selectively to the external world.

The following evening there was a knock at the kitchen door. Hogahn was lying by the woodstove and I was on the couch. He couldn't bark and he couldn't get up to go to the door. He looked at me. It was not a casual look: he stared at me. He was making sure that I understood the situation, that I was aware of his condition and the potential danger at the door. Over the next few weeks, while he was healing, he kept connected to me through that stare. In situations in which he might normally have used other motions of his body to communicate, he used his eyes.

Through the healing process, I watched him listen to his body. He was completely aware that his body could not move in its normal way. He was, in this sense, aware of his body as separate from his mind. But the idea of pitting his mind against his body in a contest of wills would have been incomprehensible to him. All of his energy went into restoring his body. The purpose at the center of his self was to bring his body and his mind back into unity.

In human spiritual development we sometimes go on an inner journey to recover a part of ourselves that has been split off and lost to us. In the shamanic tradition, we can go on a journey to recover the soul. Hogahn went on an inner journey to recover the parts of his body that had split off and were lost to him. He retrieved his body's power.

In keeping connected to their own bodies, animals keep connected to the body of the world. They feel the body of the world in the resonating response of their own bodies. For them, as for Don Juan, "the world is a feeling."

Animals resonate to the energy of a place and stay only if it feels right to them. They find the right path to take, the right direction to face, the right place to lie down. If you watch a Monk seal looking for a place to land, she swims along the beach or the reef, her large head lifted high above the water on her powerful neck, eyes and nostrils wide open, at the height of alertness. She cruises until she finds the right place to cross between ocean and land. She never just swims straight in and lands. Once she has landed, she drags and flops her great body around on the sand until she has found the right spot. Only then will she sleep. She waits until she feels the harmony between herself and the spot.

When Hogahn lost a stick, it was very hard to interest him in another one. Sometimes down at the lake, the stick he chose was rotten and when I threw it into the water it sank. He would circle the place where it disappeared, waiting for it to float to the surface again, not giving up. Knowing it was gone, I would try to distract him by throwing another stick. He ignored the other stick and kept circling. He was waiting for the energy of that stick only.

When a human is about to enter a new situation, he will use his eyes, looking carefully around, to decide if it is safe. After visual attention, he will use hearing. These two perceptual systems, vision and hearing, are distance systems. We are able to see and hear across considerable space.

When a dog is about to enter a new scene, he also looks and listens. When you open the door for a dog, he stands on the threshold for several minutes, letting in cold air in winter and mosquitoes in the spring. He sniffs the air, pulling it inside himself, to pick up smells of danger. Then, if he feels safe enough, he runs all over the space, sniffing, tasting, and touching. His whole body gets involved in the exploration of the space.

Tasting and touching are contact systems: to

taste and touch, you must let the thing come right up against your body. In touch, you tune into the warmth and pressure of the thing pushing against your skin. When an animal licks you, he is tasting and touching together, bringing you especially close.

I was a little tired and grouchy when I got to Salt Pond one day. As I walked to the beach I saw a small long-haired dog sitting about ten feet up from the water, at the highest part of the sand before it slopes down to the sea. As I got closer, I could see that she was watching two men and a large, long-haired dog swimming together. She saw me and ran to greet me excitedly.

One of the men in the water apparently felt that she was bothering me and called her to him. She ran to the water's edge but quickly retreated as a wave splashed her belly. The men and the large dog were playing in the water and soon forgot her. She came back to me, plopping her wet body on my dry towel and licking my cheek.

Although we had seen each other before, she had always been together with the men and the dog. We had never even greeted each other. Now, feeling nervous and a little abandoned, she had come to me for comfort. And I was suddenly given a burst of licking joy. I felt much better and so did she. For a few moments, the two of us were a pack.

Sometimes we just want to huddle on someone's lap. Humans have created a society in which only children and lovers do this easily. But animals will leap on your lap and lick your face whenever they feel like it. When they feel close to someone, they touch.

We have trained ourselves to love from a distance. An animal loves up close.

There are certain places that you come to—the top of a hill, the bottom of a valley, a cove of the ocean— that say, "Rest." You stay and you feel a special energy that is alive and vibrant and at the same time peaceful and centered. These are places of power. For me, these places are usually circled with rocks.

When I come to these places I want to lie down. I want to lie down with a rock just as I want to lie down with Hogahn. I want to feel the energy through my whole body. There is something about lying down that opens the body to natural power. Perhaps it is because we are not using any energy to balance, to stay standing. We relax completely into the earth's power. This power is mana, spiritual power.

When you think of nature and the energy of a rock, you can see the absurdity of the human power struggle. In the human framework, the rock would be hoarding power and trying to prevent me from taking any away. I would do the same, and the rock and I would be in a struggle for dominance. The rock would be naturally stronger and more in harmony with the surroundings, gaining strength from its connection. I, of course, being human, would find some way of "winning," like a bulldozer. I would "conquer the wilderness."

This is not how the rock or I feel. The rock freely gives me its energy, which I feel as mana. And I freely give to the rock whatever I bring—the energy of emotions, the flow of happiness over the beauty of the rock and the harmony of its surrounding space.

Contrary to all the documentaries we see about animal violence, and all of our human concepts of dominance and survival of the fittest, I know that animals live in a deep, bodily understanding of mana. They are lovingly connected to the natural world and trust it to share its power. They never hurt or destroy the earth, the holy mountain.

Animals return us to our memory of the first dance. It is dance unlimited by the walls of cultural values, before harm and rejection split off parts of the self from parts of the world. It is the happiness in our hearts of being alive, of being in harmony, of accepting and being accepted, of feeling at one with the whole.

The animal-human infant seeks to be unified with the rhythms of the universe. It wants to nurse at the body of its mother, to feel her breathing, her heartbeat, her skin. It tunes into the rhythms of her body and modulates its own rhythms. The mother holds the infant and the infant holds her.

The animal-human child dances with the energies of the universe. Her body picks up the feelings of the adults around her. She resonates to the energies of her pack or tribe. She is aware that a certain animal resonates with a great deal of mana. She is aware that a certain ritual is a gathering of mana for the tribe. She is aware because she feels the mana inside herself, at the core.

She is aware that another energy, perhaps the song of the rain, is the rhythm of peacefulness. The pack sits under a shelter and listens to the raindrops, and it is a time of quiet, of resting with the rain.

She understands that everything is connected. The rain is connected to the feeling of quiet within herself. The pack's contentment is her contentment. When she is cuddled against the adults and the other babies, and the rhythm of her breathing is in harmony with the breathing of the pack, she is happy. She feels her body's power.

IDENTIFICATION

Wʜᴇɴ a creature wants to know us, and we want to know it, there is a flowing connection. We open ourselves to each other's energy. We sense and echo each other's rhythms. We are empathically attuned.

Sea mammals such as dolphins and manatees seem to want to know us. They sense that when we swim into deep water our intention is to meet with them. We are feeling a little nervous, vulnerable in the encompassing water, but we do not close ourselves off in our vulnerability. We want to be there with them.

Fear, which is often present in the meeting between a wild animal and a human on land, can be completely absent with a sea mammal. Each knows that the other does not intend any harm. We tune into each other's energy and we feel the nervousness, the curiosity, the desire to communicate. In the similarity of feelings, we are able to feel trust.

And when there is trust, there is the miracle of feeling oneself reflected in the energy of the other.

On Kauai there are many people who feel close to dolphins. Generations of fishermen who work the dangerous waters around the island have been helped by the pods of spinner dolphins who live here. Recently an eighty-one-year-old man was wading close to the shore when a wave knocked him into the water and a strong current took him out to sea. When rescuers found him, a pod of dophins was circling him. They were protecting him from sharks by staying with him.

When people speak of their meetings with dolphins, you feel a different energy, a shift to a different reality. They may have been with the dolphins for only a few minutes, yet the encounter changed their lives. Char is a longtime resident of the island who swims regularly with dolphins. When she spoke to me, I felt as if I were back with the manatee in a magical connection.

The first time Char swam with dolphins was at Secret Beach on Kauai. A pod of spinner dolphins found her, and she was to meet with this pod many times in the years to come.

Char was afraid of sharks. She had worked with whale research groups in the waters off Kauai and had seen sharks close to her. Most of us who swim in the ocean are afraid of sharks. I meet surfers at the water's edge, coming in or going out, and our exchanges of information about the conditions of the water always include any sightings of sharks. When the current is strong or the surf is high, the more experienced surfers will stay in the water. When a shark is spotted, we all leave the water.

When Char first saw the dolphins, she saw their dorsal fins, which look just like shark fins, and she was afraid. When she saw their faces, the unmistakable dolphin eyes and mouth, a gentle half-smile, she relaxed a little. The dolphins, about ten of them, started swimming in a circle around her. Perhaps they sensed her fear and wanted to give her their protection. They created a field of sonar energy vibrating around her. The energy surged through her body, flooding her with sound. "I was breathless from excitement, and yet I could breathe more deeply than I've ever breathed before," Char said. "The only way I can describe the feeling is ecstasy. It was a mutual thing. We tuned into each other."

A few years later Char was pregnant. She had been swimming with the dolphins many times, but while she was pregnant with Michael, she had two extraordinary meetings with them.

The first meeting did not happen on Kauai, but off the Big Island, where she and her husband, Larry, were visiting. Early that morning, they'd gone down to a bay where they had heard that dolphins were swimming. They were with a friend who was not sure he really wanted to find any dolphins. When Char wants to let dolphins know she is present, she chants. She chanted now as she and Larry entered the water. Their friend was struggling with his mask and flippers and stayed behind to adjust them.

They swam out, about two hundred feet from shore, and she and Larry met the dolphins. The dolphins were moving in small groups of about four each, and she and Larry became separated from each other by about a hundred feet. And then, when she was alone with them, a group of seven dolphins, three nursing mothers, three babies, and one other, came around her. They were nursing as they swam, and they let her swim with them. "I was so honored that they would let me swim with them," Char said. "I could cry just thinking about it."

Larry never saw the nursing dolphins. And their friend, who entered the water just a few minutes behind them, did not see a single dolphin. The dolphins chose not to find him.

The second meeting during Char's pregnancy was amazing because of something that happened not with Char, but with her dog, Beluga. Beluga was raised close to the ocean and is at home there. She is part yellow Lab, an excellent swimmer. She had been with Char on other swims.

Char was eight and a half months pregnant when she, Larry, and Beluga went to Secret Beach. The two humans and the dog swam out to sea. When they reached deep water, about three hundred feet from shore, the dolphins found them.

In the calmly rolling ocean, there were one

hundred and twenty spinner dolphins and the three nondolphins who'd gone out to meet them. The dolphins were on all sides and below them. Thinking about the manatee, I asked if Char had touched one of the dolphins.

"They stayed just out of reach," she said. "Even if you could have touched them, you wouldn't have," she said. "It was a very respectful space."

The sense of touch came from the energy of water and sound. The energy was unbelievable. "Sound permeated my whole abdomen," she said.

Char was totally relaxed with the dolphins. She was floating, letting the energy that filled the space flow through her. She was part of the pod.

And then Beluga and four dolphins swam out to sea. The five creatures just took off together. "There were five animals out there—one dog and four dolphins," Char said.

Beluga was lying quietly near us and I went to sit with her. I wanted to know what had happened when she was alone with the dolphins. I looked into her eyes and talked to her. She told me that she was a calm, wise dog. She dismissed my other questions as unanswerable.

When I think about Beluga and the four dolphins, I feel deeply happy and confirmed in my sense of basic connections. Beluga initially swam out with Char and Larry because they were her pack. Hogahn often follows me into the water, and when I go far from shore he always comes out to find me. But when Beluga left Char and Larry, she was

leaving her pack. She must have been very comfortable, very free of any fear for their or her own
safety. She must have been feeling the same energy,
the same connectedness, as Char. When the dolphins signaled that they wanted to go off, she went
with them easily. We, as humans, have all kinds of
intellectual knowledge about dolphins; we know
they will not hurt us. But Beluga only knew what
she felt and experienced at that moment. She knew
the absence of all fear. She felt the sense of complete
belonging.

"It was a three-species day," Char said.

The closeness between sea mammals and humans
continues to amaze me. Fishermen learn to negoti-
ate difficult motions from watching seals. One day I
watched a fisherman retrieving a net at the base of
a cliff on Kauai. He was fishing at the far end of Salt
Pond, where the waves are not broken by any reef
and come crashing into the rocks with dangerous
energy. He climbed down the cliff and stood for a
moment, holding on to a rock and watching the
rhythm of the water. Then he got down on his belly
on the flattest rock and crawled into the water.
When the water swelled, he gathered the net; when
the waves broke, he went under them. There were
five silver fish caught inside the net. With the net
gathered and close against his body, he let a wave
take him back to the flat rock, then crawled out of

the water. He moved in and out of the turbulent water on his belly, just like a seal.

When I was a child my mother used to take me to the Central Park Zoo. I had conflicting feelings about the zoo, wanting to see the animals and wanting to open the locks and cages and set them free. The seals were kept in a concrete pond, under the sky, and they were usually swimming. Although I knew that they too were trapped, I didn't feel the same sadness. I watched them swim as I watched human dancers, feeling the motion. The other animals, the bears and the monkeys, could not run and leap as they would have in the wilderness. But in the pool, the seals were able to dive and roll somewhat as they would have in the ocean. I felt the energy of happiness in their movements.

Now, I look out at the ocean around Kauai and I feel the amazing freedom of the seals, the whales, and the dolphins. They swim great distances, especially the whales, migrating with the seasons. All of the ocean is their home; they don't have water boundaries.

Dogen, a Zen master, wrote:

> When a fish swims, it swims on and on, and there is no end to the water. When a bird flies, it flies on and on, and there is no end to the sky. . . . Thus, they use all of it at every moment, and in every place they have perfect freedom.

When a humpback whale is spotted far out in the channel, everyone gets up to look. Men and women stand on top of pickup trucks and lift their children onto their shoulders to give them a better view. The whale lifts its great body from the water like lightning breaking from a stormy sky. Everyone on the shore feels the power and freedom in the humpback's leap. Everyone feels, for a moment, connected to mana.

We on the land, animal and human, have to mark off our territories in order to feel safe. I am not speaking about greed—owning great quantities of land and keeping others out—but simple survival, needing a piece of land to live on. The land is always being divided by its residents, relatively peacefully by animals and not so peacefully by humans. Sometimes I feel that the island is a zoo, with all of us marking off our cages.

The ocean is constantly moving: swaying and flowing. It does not stay still for easy boundaries. At the bottom, creatures have their own spaces; an eel may have its sanctuary in the hollow of a reef. But for the sea mammals, and most of the fish, sanctuary is the water, the whole ocean. They would not divide the water any more than birds would divide the air. When we see them from our spots on the shore, gliding and leaping across the wide water, we feel a deep freedom. Space, for them, is boundless.

Yet the closeness between us is far more powerful than any differences. One day I was privileged to witness a Hawaiian Monk seal's exploration of a human smell. It was a tiny, simple event, but it was an exquisite image of her sense of us.

Monk seals live in the waters around Kauai, and some of the time on the land. The pups are born on the land, in rookeries at the edges of the islands. For the rest of her life the seal feels safe on the land. When she is tired, she hauls herself onto the shore and enters a deep sleep which can last many hours. Like a bird, she crosses easily between worlds.

The Salt Pond coastline covers a great deal of land and water. At one end is the mouth of the Hanapepe River and the harbor. After the harbor the land bulges into a wide peninsula of volcanic rock, the place where the fisherman gathered his net. As this peninsula curves back around, a reef begins. It starts as a low shelf coming gradually out of the water, and then rises, stretching along the coastline and ending as the protective enclosure of a gentle bay with a sandy beach.

It was low tide, and the seal was swimming where the reef was above the water. She edged along the high reef, stretching her neck, searching for an opening. When she came to the shelf, she looked around and hauled herself up.

She waddled along the shelf, moving like an inchworm, arching her middle and then pushing her whole body forward as it flattened out. As she arched, her flippers reached down to the reef on each side, keeping her round slippery body from rolling over. She pushed about ten feet onto the shelf, flopping around until she found the right spot, and lay down.

Her sleek brown body, still wet from the ocean, looked exactly like a rock still wet from the tide. As it dried out, her fur became gray, with bits of white visible in the bright sun. Then she looked exactly like a rock dried to gray by the heat of the sun.

She was away from the beach, away from the places where people swim and meet each other, but after a while a girl of about twelve wandered by. She walked in a calm, easy manner along the line where the tide had deposited millions of tiny bones and shells from the sea. She moved rhythmically, lightly, head bent slightly, focused on the tideline for shells to take home with her. She was wearing white sneakers.

The tideline was two feet inland from the shelf, seven feet from the sleeping seal. The girl could almost have touched the seal if she had seen it. But it looked, of course, exactly like a gray rock on a gray reef. The girl walked by, passing the seal and passing me, without looking up.

Now the tide, which had been gently lapping the edges of the shelf, began rolling farther and farther onto the reef. I watched as a large wave pushed itself up to the seal's side.

She stirred, opening one eye, raising her head and her flippers. She scratched her nose. Waddling away from the encroaching water and up to the soft sand, she stopped right on the old tideline, just where the girl had recently walked. Under her nose was a footprint left by the girl's sneaker.

She put her nose down and sniffed the pattern. Then she waddled along the line of sneaker prints, taking her time and carefully sniffing each indentation. She examined ten footprints before she plopped down on the last print and went to sleep.

The seal had interrupted her deep sleep to make an exploration of a girl's footprints. I tried to imagine the smells she was getting. There would be rubber from the sneaker bottom, clots of red dirt clinging between the ridges, and bits of decaying plants and animals mixed with the fragrant earth. There would be the human foot-smell: sweaty, pungent, and salty, flavors of living and dead skin. She must have liked it, or she would have moved away. Instead, she slept on it.

She was curious about us, and I had the rare privilege of watching her exploration. And she liked us; at least she liked the smell of our feet. I had an enormous desire to crawl up next to her and go to sleep.

For almost two years I watched Monk seals sleeping on the land and fantasized about meeting one in the water. And then, just recently, it happened.

I was swimming in the bay at Salt Pond when a Monk seal entered. We were both in the water, about twenty feet apart, when our eyes first met. I was close to the reef and I moved slowly onto its ledge to make room for her to pass. After watching me to see that I was out of the way, she swam by me to the beach, looking for a place to land.

It was a beautiful, clear day and lots of people were on the beach. A very small child was standing in the water, and the seal was drawn toward her. She swam in, coming within a few feet of the little girl, sniffing her. The child's mother, who had been sitting quietly, jumped up to get a camera and ran back excitedly snapping pictures. The seal was comfortable with the child and might have landed, but when the mother came back she turned away. She cruised along the beach, only to find more people who were running down to see her. It was not a restful scene. She turned back to the open water and went under.

Everyone assumed that the seal had left the bay. The lifeguard returned to his chair, people walked away, and I slipped off the reef and into the water. I swam across to the far, deserted side of the bay.

I was filled with the energy of seeing the seal, of seeing her wanting to explore the child, of having her look into my eyes, and I swam with unusual power. I got to the other side of the bay without effort and without looking up. When I stopped, about twenty feet from the far end, I opened my eyes and there she was. She had come across underwater and was watching the sand for the right place to land.

I froze in the water. I was not near enough to

any part of the reef to climb up, and she was between me and the shore. I stayed as still as I could
in the water, hoping that she would climb onto the
sand. When she was safely resting, I would circle
around and land.

Of course, she sensed me behind her in the water. She turned around very startled. I was between
her and the opening in the reef that leads out of the
bay. She swam toward me.

We were about six feet from each other, our
heads both up, staring at each other. There was
nothing in the world except water, sky, and our two
heads. There was no place to hide. Running away
was not a possibility. We were just there, two creatures looking into each other's eyes.

On land, face-to-face with a large wild animal,
there is always the thought that you can run, get
behind a tree, find a weapon. On land you are surrounded by your familiar objects, your familiar
thoughts. In the ocean you are just there, your small
body and puny swimming ability and her great body
and powerful water-motion. You face her stripped
of human pretensions, human cunning. You face
her as just yourself.

Everything both of you are feeling bounces
back and forth between you. I felt some fear, from
both of us, because we had startled each other. I also
felt intense interest from both of us: who is this creature with its head above the water like mine, its eyes
like mine? I felt the incredible connection of recognition: this seal looked like my father.

This kind of encounter shifts your awareness. It sends you into nonordinary reality, where a seal and your father are somehow the same. When you come back to the land and the ordinary world, you carry forever this awareness.

Talking with Kaleo, one of the lifeguards on Kauai, I told him about my meeting in the water with the seal, leaving out the part about my father. He said he had a friend who'd also met a Monk seal face-to-face in the water. "And you know what he thought in that first moment, when he first saw it?" he asked. "He thought it was his wife." We laughed together, and then I told him about seeing my father. We laughed some more, and within the laughter was the feeling of truth.

I wonder whom the Monk seal was seeing when she headed straight for the small child on the beach. Did she see a seal baby? I wonder whom she saw when she turned in the water and I was there.

The sculptor Louise Nevelson said: "Each individual has awareness for the things they truly identify with. Identification is love." There is a strong sense of identification between us and the Monk seals, between us and the dolphins and whales. For a moment, in the middle of the ocean, we see in them a person-creature whom we love. For a moment, we recognize a creature who sees into our soul. When a creature wants to know us, we want to be known.

SHAMANIC JOURNEY

I have always thought of beige as the ultimate color of camouflage. I know that this is only one vision, one way of merging. I can see that the ocean water changes constantly from transparent green, to deep blue, to the muddy red after a storm—not beige at all. I see that the volcanic rocks along the shore range from dry gray to wet black, like Monk seals, as the tides and sun brush across their surface. I see, as you enter the Hanapepe Valley, that the koa trees above and the taro plants below enclose you in a sphere of green feathers, a million leafy roosters flapping their wings.

Still, perhaps because the desert kept me safe as a child, I visualize reality as sand. In the shamanic journey I want to tell you about, the land had the feeling of the desert and the animal who came to guide me was the color of sand. She was a lion.

On a shamanic journey the seeker goes to another reality to find understanding. When the journey begins, the shaman, or the person who comes to the shaman for help, is in need of some necessary awareness. The seeker can be confused and even troubled. In some cases, the person has lost touch with the core of the self and the journey is undertaken to reconnect the parts of the self to the soul.

For these reasons, the seeker needs a spiritual guide, someone who knows the territory. In one of the many intricate and beautiful variations on the shamanic journey, Dante travels to heaven and hell and finds Beatrice as his guide. In traditional shamanic cultures, the guiding being is an animal. This animal, like Kirby with Anna, knows his way in the other reality. In traditional shamanic cultures this other reality is deeply connected to the natural world—the wind and the water, the mountains and the moon; the natural world *is* the spiritual world and we are all spiritual beings. It makes complete sense for the guide in the spiritual-natural world to be an animal.

My shamanic journey took place while I was trying to decide what to do with myself, where to flop my body down, for the next few years. I was thinking mainly in terms of the need for shelter, for a tiny piece of land with a little house where animals could live with me and no one would bother us.

As I entered the other world, the lion was waiting for me. I had never seen her before, but it was clear that she was my guide. She was standing on a large rock, her beige fur gleaming in sunlight.

Her eyes also were beige, but they were the clear beige of Amber, the fish who let me feel forgiveness at the barrier reef.

The lion was beige and amber but her surroundings were not exclusively beige: the mountains were dusty purple and the stones around us were a deep, thick gray. She was the purity from which these other colors emerged. It seemed that she had made the other parts of the world distinct in order that I might see them, and that when I was gone they would all return to beige again.

She leapt down from the rock and, standing close to me, let me know that her body was real. She rested a large, heavy paw on my leg and I pressed my hand into the fur of her thick, solid neck. The strands of our fur-hair fell together. Then she informed me, from the center of her real body, that my body could be weightless. *You do not need a patch of land or a house*, she told me. *Your body will float.*

She led me into the air, where we floated, intentional clouds. We landed on a ledge high on the side of the mountain. Peering from the mouth of the cave at the back of the ledge were her cubs. They emerged, all amber-beige, to greet me, waddling excitedly, bumbling and flopping all over themselves in happiness. I lay down and let them smell and lick me. Then their mother took me back, floating, to the rock where we had met, and I returned to my normal world.

After this journey I was able to let go of my fear of not owning a house, not owning a piece of land, not having a place that was exclusively mine. This need had been strong in me for many years, and it was a great relief to let it go. The lion showed me that in the places where I will land, there will be babies, maybe puppies, maybe my granddaughter Siena, new generations of life. In the places where I will land there will be belonging and love.

I said that the lion's body was real, and it was, but her body was also a vision in an unusual state of awareness, an image in my mind. The trick is being able to see both kinds of awareness as real. In teaching the shamanic tradition of Huna, Serge King speaks of four levels, four of many ways that we can approach reality, which I have found very helpful.

On the first level we are all bodies and objects, separate and physical. This is the usual way of looking at the world, Don Juan's "ordinary reality."

On the second level, we tune into energies and gather information, from our perceptual systems, from empathy, from mental awareness. We are separate centers, in touch with each other.

On the third level, we see the connectedness of everything.

On the fourth level, everything is one.

The shaman moves freely between these different ways of seeing. When action is required, the shaman moves on the level which makes the most sense in that moment, the level that works.

Looking at animals from this framework, it seems to me that they also move freely between the levels. When they are protecting each other and themselves, they are acting at the bodily level (level 1). They are protecting their separate, physical bodies from external, separate danger.

In this same situation, however, they can also be at the third level, feeling their connection to each other. They see that danger to the other is danger to the self. They protect the separate body (level 1) out of connectedness (level 3).

And they are always living their awareness at level 2, in a state of attunement. They stay aware of all the energies, checking things out.

The fourth level is pure spiritual awareness. It is probably the case that as with humans, some animals see this way more than others.

So animals move fluidly from one level to another, and in the same moment are seeing the levels together, in parallel. And this makes sense, because the levels are only ways of separating things so that we can understand them; they are helpful explanatory categories. Animals see and feel the levels in harmony.

Animals and shamans see on all levels and see the harmony between the levels. When the lion and I were together, her body and my body were real, separate bodies, and we were intimately connected. When the lion and I were together in this other reality, our bodies were also cloud-bodies, able to float. In harmony, things that seem to be in opposition can flow side by side, in and around, because of our awareness.

Animals are tuned exquisitely to harmony. Awareness of harmony is awareness of the energy of the whole. Animals live essentially in harmony. They are most in touch with themselves, most alive, most safe, in a world of harmony.

Harmony is the normal, natural condition of the universe for animals. They do not live in fear; they do not live with an image of the world as dangerous. They do not have the human idea that some malevolent, evil spirit is out to get them. The world feels essentially safe and animals are essentially peaceful and happy.

Animals live in connection to their world. When something, even the smallest thing, begins to change, they stay aware. If the change brings a feeling that something is wrong, they listen to their feeling. Disharmony, at the level of feeling, is just this sense that something is wrong, that something is happening that doesn't belong. The animal separates itself from the part that doesn't belong. There is disconnection between the animal and the world.

Staying connected is tuning into all feelings, including the sense that something is wrong. Staying connected means staying, as long as necessary, with awareness of separation and disharmony.

At exactly the right moment, the animal acts to

restore harmony. This means acting to save itself, to save its babies, to save its companions, animal and human. It acts to restore a safe world for everyone.

Harmony at a personal level is the feeling of belonging. It is the sense of peacefulness when the energy inside you and the energy around you flow together. It is, ultimately, the sense of connection. Restoring harmony is returning to the peacefulness you feel when everything is connected. It is seeing the world again as whole.

I think that humans feel the same flow between harmony and disharmony, but for some of us the proportions are reversed. A lot of the time we feel disharmony: stress, anxiety, something wrong. And then there are the moments of harmony, which in different spiritual traditions we call love, enlightenment, and pure awareness. I think that animals live most of their time in enlightenment.

The summer before I taught the course in theories of the self, I was living on City Island with Douglas, Joanna, Muky, and Sasha. I had made a commitment to teach this new course, and one of the theories my students needed for their professional development was object relations theory. In synchrony, Joanna was taking a course in just this theory. At night we would sit at the kitchen table, trying to make sense of the mental density. Muky and Sasha followed our voices like music, enjoying the rhythms as they flowed from contemplation to frustration to occasional breakthroughs of understanding. Ponderous sound waves vibrated through the warm summer air and echoed in their ears. When Joanna said the word "schizoid," Muky rolled over happily.

If you ever want to go crazy, object relations theory is a good place to start. It was developed by several psychiatrists working independently, who used different names for the same concepts because they liked to feel distinct from one another. One night Joanna and I were suffering more acutely than usual over a book by Harry Guntrip: *Schizoid phenomena, object-relations, and the self*. Muky listened to the disharmony, watched us go off to bed, and then chewed Guntrip up. He didn't destroy the entire book; he just put enough holes in the theory to shift our awareness. From then on, we took from the theory what we felt was connected to our inner understanding and left the rest. When we hear the word "schizoid," Muky and I roll on the floor together.

I am not against theory or the intricacies of human language. Through human language, Anna was able to tell her children about her dying, and later, again through language, Eileen was able to remember and accept her mother's dying. Their stories were theories, giving structure and coherence to the fragments of feelings and images they had stored. Putting their

232

experiences into language gave them deeper understanding, and with that understanding, they felt
clear and peaceful at the core of themselves.

I am only against theories and stories that limit
our understanding of the universe. There is a set of
theories in philosophy and psychology which insist
that we can never know another creature's mind.
These theories maintain that when we mistakenly
think we know something, we have actually used
inductive reasoning, a guess based upon the person's present behavior and our own past experience.
We see a man grimace. We hear a tight, strained
tone in his voice. We see him clench his fist. We
induce from these clues that he is angry.

Our own feelings, according to these theories,
are not any more directly experienced than the
feelings of others. We perceive that our heart is
beating faster and our jaw muscles are clenched.
We perceive that we are in a particular situation,
one that we don't like. We induce from the combination of bodily and situational clues that we
must be angry.

I have always been uncomfortable with this
story, sensing that something was definitely wrong
with it. I *knew* sometimes that I was not guessing.
But the theory was able to explain so many situations in our human relationships: all the times when
someone has been upset and we haven't known it;
when someone was angry at us and we didn't see it
until much later; when someone is able to keep a

significant part of her life a secret from us. And it explained our confusion about ourselves: the times when someone is hurting us and we feel numb. Later we realize how angry we were, but we were unaware of our own feelings in the moment.

One evening, thinking about shamanic awareness, I suddenly understood. The inductive reasoning theory is perfectly good, wonderfully explanatory, in the framework of ordinary reality. And this is the reality, the world of ordinary human society, in which most of us live much of our time. We block off awareness of another's upsettedness because we don't want to deal with it. Dealing with it would mean acting impeccably, with perhaps serious consequences. A child comes to us in fear, and instead of opening to the fear and joining with the child, we think and say that everything is fine. We shut off our awareness.

The theory of inductive reasoning actually makes sense if our experience is limited to the world of ordinary reality. Without awareness, we have to guess.

All of us, however, have lived in nonordinary reality. We have been to other levels of awareness. We have felt connected to another being at the core of ourselves. We have acted from deep certainty in the face of danger. We have been in touch with ourselves at the same time as we have been in touch with the energy of the universe.

In nonordinary reality, in the state of aware-

ness, there is connectedness and there is understanding. Here, inductive reasoning is completely
unnecessary. When you are aware, you don't guess.
That is why, for many years, the theory bothered
me. Now I understand that these philosophers and
psychologists have been trapped in a one-level
world. To their credit, they have developed an explanation that works on this limited level rather
well. But there are many other levels of awareness.

In the *Ashtavakra Gita* it is said:

> Your nature is pure awareness.

The path of animal connections which I have tried
to describe is a path of deepening awareness. The
spiritual journey is a journey of healing connection
and awareness.

The path of animal connections brings a deepening awareness of motion and rest. You breathe,
stretch, reach, walk, hop, leap, swim, float, fly, land,
and lie down. On this path you are your body. You
move with the rhythms around you. You respond
to the fragrance of a flower by breathing it in, letting
it inside you, becoming one with it. The rhythm of
the air touches and enters your body. The ground
returns the touch of your step: it contacts you on the
soles of your feet.

The path of animal connections brings a deepening awareness of inner motion and stillness. You feel peaceful, happy, nervous, fearful, playful, serious, light, heavy, centered, uncentered, in touch, out of touch, clear, foggy, trapped, and free. On this path you are your emotions. Sometimes you feel a deep stillness at the heart of yourself.

And most especially, on this path that I am describing, you feel your connection to animals. This is the path of human-animal love. On this path, you tune into the feelings of an animal. You respond to the happiness of an animal by vibrating with the energy, feeling the happiness, becoming happy.

From feeling happy with an animal, you gain a deeper awareness of your own happiness. When you and an animal are together in the feeling of happiness, echoing the happiness between you, the feeling takes on a new richness and depth. Pure happiness echoes within and between you.

When you are experiencing the fragrance of a flower, the motion of your own body, or the happiness of an animal, you are experiencing awareness. When you are tuned in, completely focused, you are one with the fragrance, the motion, the happiness. What are you, your self, at that moment? You are the awareness. The core of your self is your awareness.

The nature of animals is pure awareness. Our own nature, too, is pure awareness.

The path of animal connections is, like most spiritual paths, essentially nonverbal. Geetel Sussman, who does healing work on Kauai, studied in the Philippines with a powerful healer. Her training was all nonverbal: she did not know the healer's language. She said that part of her training was to see what she was seeing, to feel what she was feeling, without being able to ask questions. She had to shed her Western framework. Her questions could only have come from the first level, the level of separate bodies and verbal categories. But the transformations she witnessed could only be understood at the third and fourth levels of nonordinary reality. She meditated and prayed a lot, and in the silence, she shifted her awareness.

A friend, D, described the essence of animal-human communication after her dog Biko died of lung cancer. Biko came to her wild and fearful, a dog who did not belong, tipping over D's garbage can in the middle of the night for her only meal. Eventually, Biko stayed with D. "Biko recognized me. Her emotional past was really mine," D said.

"Biko and I talked to each other in thought language," she told me. "With humans, the conscious mind often blocks our inner understanding. With an animal, there is no way to confuse the intuitive message that you get—first the fear, then the trust, then the love. Love is always there. Animals are about love."

Edgar Bourque, a priest of the Augustinians of the Assumption, used to talk to me about love. He understood the journey from ordinary to spiritual reality as a journey of love. I think that when he entered the spiritual world, the feeling at the core of himself was the feeling of love. Spiritual reality was the world of pure and eternal love.

In New England after a snowstorm, the sun comes out and the trees and ground and houses and ponds are all shining in whiteness. You walk outside and you feel a deep happiness at being alive. You feel awe in the presence of such beauty, and privileged to be part of this incredible setting. It stretches out like the night sky, sunlight touching snow in every direction. In this world you feel happy and blessed just to be alive. You feel the connectedness, the oneness of everything. You feel love for everything.

I think that animals feel this boundless love. Everything is full of wonder, everything makes them happy. Everything is an adventure in being alive.

When the first snowstorm arrived each year in New England Panda and I would sit at the window and watch it gather. Then early the next morning we would go out and roll in the snow. It felt like a new world. Everything was clear and shining and completely white. Everything felt connected. We were just ourselves in the deep soft snow.

The theologian and poet Thomas Merton said:

> There is in all things an inexhaustible sweetness and purity, a silence that is a fountain of action and joy. It rises up in wordless gentleness and flows out to me from unseen roots of all created being.

I felt inexhaustible sweetness and purity from Panda, from Hogahn, and from all the animals. And they felt the sweetness and purity in everything around them. They found sweetness and purity in all of us. When they resonated to our centers they brought us back in touch with the sweetness and purity in ourselves.

I felt wordless gentleness in all the animals. I found it in Hogahn and Panda, in Neti-Neti and the Monk seal, in Amber and the cane spider. In the water with the manatees, I was immersed in wordless gentleness.

Each of these stories is a shamanic journey. Some were major transformations and some were small moments of love and awareness. In all of the journeys, an animal was there to guide.

I understand very deeply that I am an animal. The differences between Hogahn and me are unimportant. He is wiser in certain ways, I in others. He needs my help for certain things, and I need his. We are there for each other.

If this is your path, the animals will teach you.